SAMPLERS FOR THE NURSERY & CHILDREN'S ROOMS

SAMPLERS FOR THE NURSERY & CHILDREN'S ROOMS

DEBORAH ANN MURPHY

With Beverley Zadikoff

Fleming H. Revell Company
Old Tappan, New Jersey

"Antique" lowercase alphabet used in the Baby Blanket used by permission of Leisure Arts, Little Rock, AR.

Scripts used in Train Up a Child and Pippa Passes and alphabet used in Little Lamb used by permission of Jean Farish Needleworks.

Library of Congress Catologing-in-Publication Data

Murphy, Deborah Ann.
    Samplers for the nursery and children's rooms / Deborah Ann Murphy with Beverley Zadikoff.
        p.   cm.
    Bibliography: p.
    ISBN 0-8007-1623-X : $8.95
    1. Cross-stitch—Patterns. 2. Samplers. I. Zadikoff, Beverley. II. Title.
TT778.C76M87 1989
746.3—dc19

89-3826
CIP

Copyright © 1990 by Deborah Ann Murphy
Published by the Fleming H. Revell Company
Old Tappan, New Jersey 07675
Printed in the United States of America

To Gene and Patrick, once again, with love.

Eternal gratitude to all the generous stitchers who made this book possible: Beth Murphy, Beverley Zadikoff, Barbara Traum, Barbie Hemberger, and Betty McAlpin.

Special thanks to the editorial, art, and production departments of Fleming H. Revell Company, for their support, creativity, and enthusiasm.

And to my parents, Ann and Scott Dunbar.

But above all this book is dedicated to my friend and partner, Beverley Zadikoff, with love and thanks for her patience, her tireless attention to detail, her sense of humor, and her wonderful ideas.

D. A. Murphy

Contents

Preface

The recent explosion of interest in cross-stitch samplers has led to a burgeoning need for charted sampler designs. Many of the charts already available are reproductions of original samplers, both American and English.

In our book we present a collection of wholly original designs, based on traditional sampler compositions, themes, and motifs. Some of our patterns are strikingly contemporary. Others closely resemble their familiar forebears. In every case we have used at least one of the elements that characterize and identify samplers: alphabets, numbers, borders, wording, name or initials of the stitcher, and date of completion. We have also devoted a section at the back of the book to these individual elements, so that today's stitcher may create a unique, personal sampler.

Some of our designs may be used as birth announcements; others celebrate children's development and their relationship to the world. At least one can be stitched by children, and all have been designed to be used in the nursery or children's rooms.

Many of the finest samplers from the past were stitched by children. Our book is devoted to children and the people who love them.

Introduction: Samplers—A Historical Note

A sampler is a self-contained piece of embroidery, usually executed on evenweave fabric (see page 15), that contains examples of characters (numbers and letters) and motifs, in random, bordered, and horizontally banded compositions. Samplers are usually dated and initialed by the stitcher, and often contain prayers, mottoes, or aphorisms. At their most mechanical they are exercises in dexterity; at their most meaningful, samplers become expressions of timeless devotion.

While experts differ in their opinions as to the origin and age of the earliest sampler, all agree that samplers began as a means of recording embroidery stitches. Our English word *exampler* or *sampler* comes from the Latin word *exemplum*, meaning "model" or "pattern to be worked by copying or imitating." Many early samplers were long, narrow pieces of fabric, rolled (sometimes on ivory rods) and kept in a drawer or basket. On this cloth the lady of the house noted embroidery stitches by working them in complete and incomplete stages, to show her method.

She could refer to her sampler in order to remind herself of how to do a stitch or use it as a teaching aid to show others, perhaps her daughters or sisters-in-law. Often, to economize, she cut the fabric across the width of a swatch of fabric being used for another project, in a strip as narrow as seven or nine inches. With selvages at top and bottom, she entered stitches and characters as closely together as possible, to save room, and often repeated them in slightly varied forms.

Early samplers were not meant to be displayed but rather represented accumulated stitching experience and could be referred to over a lifetime and passed on to the next generation. Often, the characters stitched were distinctive markings for linens and clothing for the household. Successive generations made these very practical letters and numbers more and more elaborate, until the stitching became a decorative embellishment rather than a way to identify and keep track of linens.

Generally, the earliest samplers are arrayed with random markings, stitches, and characters. Later, horizontal banding of numbers and letters, perhaps surrounded by some random patterns, became conventional.

Rectangular and square samplers appeared in the eighteenth century as children, particularly girls, were schooled in embroidery, reading, and arithmetic. Largely a luxury for the well-to-do, schools in the eighteenth century inculcated the practice of stitching letters and numbers to imprint the lesson on a child's mind and refine it through usage. The precise and painstaking repetition of each character, at home or at school, also resulted in attractive pieces of needlework that parents could display prominently in their home showing a girl's prowess to would-be suitors. Embroidery skills were valued highly in women and showed preparedness for matrimony and the domestic responsibilities that would follow. Those samplers made at the average home were usually stitched in inexpensive, subdued colors, in cotton or wool, while girls whose parents could afford to send them to school used brilliantly colored threads of silk, linen, wool, metallics, and perhaps beads. In general, the fabrics used in early samplers were linen, wool, "linsey-woolsey" (a blend of wool and flax), "tiffany" (fine muslin), "tammy" (wool) and occasionally silk.

The advent of printed designs heralded an explosion of sampler work, as more people had access to patterns. Instead of relying on stitched work passed hand to hand, students could now see patterns and their steps on paper. In order to transfer the printed motifs, tiny puncture holes were made with a sharp needle around the shape of the pattern, and then charcoal dust was sprinkled on the paper, resulting in a fine, gray outline on the fabric beneath. This "pouncing" enabled the stitcher to transfer any printed pattern onto fabric, but resulted inevitably in the premature destruction of many books.

By the nineteenth century cross-stitch predominated over other embroidery stitches in samplers, although such stitches as the backstitch, Algerian eye, French knot, satin stitch and square stitch continued to be used for texture and pattern. The use of cross-stitch and the wide availability of counted-thread patterns enabled stitchers to faithfully reproduce characters and motifs without having to transfer them. This was easier and less destructive, although it also tended to quell the exquisite and imaginative use of the free-form embroidery stitches that had enlivened samplers since the fifteenth century. In addition, many of the delicate curvilinear designs taken from Italian lace and Indian and Chinese weaving became rather geometric in counted work. This stylistic change tended to make very much clearer the hitherto rather subtle difference between embroidery and samplers. Where embroidery could adorn furniture and clothing in a limitless, easily adaptable way, samplers tended to become free-standing works of decorative art with an aesthetic rather than practical function.

In mid-eighteenth-century America, imaginative and colorful work in samplers proliferated. Brides-to-be, wives, and teachers from England and Europe brought with them treasured patterns, and once introduced into the everyday life of Americans, these much-copied characters and motifs took on a unique New World look. American stitchers were less constrained by symmetry and formality and loved bright colors and varied stitches. In this land the stylized people, animals, objects, and buildings depicted in samplers from other countries became enlivened and combined with horizontally banded alphabets and numbers, and borders that framed the sampler were introduced.

For centuries samplers had included at least one of the following elements: the stitcher's initials, date of birth, date of completion, teacher's name, city or country of origin, an aphorism, prayer, proverb, poem, or sentiment. In America the wording became more personally descriptive; often it memorialized a dead relative (as in a mourning sampler), or the birthday of a new member of the family (family-tree samplers), sometimes it left unworked areas to be filled in by successive generations. Political themes were popular, with eagles, flags, maps, and dedications to politicians (celebrated in life or mourned in death) abounding.

Throughout the history of samplers, a common theme emerges: the central role of religion in the stitchers' lives. Almost all wording referred in some part to God, to His bounty, His omnipotence, or His blessings. Many samplers can be considered expressions of religious devotion and are dedicated to Christian life and its precepts. Today we continue to stitch samplers to express our faith and our heritage. We still include birthdays, mottoes, letters, numbers, and borders in samplers that enhance our homes and our lives. And we still consider our stitching skills sharpened by the meticulous execution of charted patterns that we share with friends and family and that we are pleased to carefully preserve for future generations.

SAMPLERS FOR THE NURSERY & CHILDREN'S ROOMS

1
A Guide to Stitching Samplers

For centuries samplers have been produced using a variety of embroidery stitches, but cross-stitch has predominated since the nineteenth century. In *Samplers for the Nursery and Children's Rooms* we have used cross-stitch for the bulk of our designs and Algerian eye, French knots, backstitches and satin stitches for detail and pattern. The following instructions will enable even those who have never threaded a needle to stitch from our charts. In addition we have provided instructional information about basic materials and techniques so that the stitcher will feel informed about making choices when buying supplies. A list of fabrics and threads is given in Appendix III, while some information about retail sources, associations, guilds, periodicals, and magazines devoted to cross-stitch appears in Appendix II.

Evenweave

Cross-stitch is a surface embroidery technique that consists of making an X, with two passes of a needle, onto evenweave fabric (*see* Illustration 1).

Evenweave fabric may be identified by its characteristic even number of warp (vertical) and weft (horizontal) threads in a given area (*see* Illustration 2).

Many evenweave fabrics are woven particularly for cross-stitch (linen, Aida, davos, and floba, for example), but evenly woven fabric found in fabric stores may also be used for cross-stitching. The importance of the even weave is that the X of each stitch will be symmetrical and when counted from a graph will exactly duplicate the proportions of the original design (*see* Illustration 3).

Calculating Finished Size

The number of threads per inch determines the finished size of any counted work—the smaller the number of threads per inch, the bigger the design; the larger the number of threads per inch, the smaller the finished design (*see* Illustration 4). So it is crucial to know two things whenever stitching from a chart: the number of stitches in the design and the number of threads per inch in the fabric of choice (*see* Illustration 5).

By referring to the Evenweave Computation Chart on page 16 you can calculate the size of any pattern on any given evenweave fabric. By knowing the size, the stitcher can be assured that it will fit a cut piece and not run off the edges. Where linen or linenlike weaves are used, remember to halve the count, since you will have to use two threads for each stitch. If you wish to use a different border from the one included in a basic chart, do not forget to change your stitch count if necessary; we have provided all border designs

15

EVENWEAVE COMPUTATION CHART
(TO DETERMINE DESIGN AREA ONLY)

STITCH COUNT OF DESIGN • LENGTH & WIDTH (add 6" to design area figure before cutting fabric)

STITCH COUNT FOR FABRIC	20	25	30	35	40	45	50	55	60	65	70	75	80	85	90	95	100	105
Herta 6	3⅜	4⅛	5	5⅞	6¾	7½	8⅜	9⅛	10	10⅞	11¾	12½	13⅜	14⅛	15	15⅞	16¾	17½
Aida 8	2½	3⅛	3¾	4⅜	5	5⅝	6¼	6⅞	7½	8⅛	8¾	9⅜	10	10⅝	11¼	11⅞	12½	13⅛
Aida 11	1⅞	2¼	2¾	3⅛	3⅝	4⅛	4½	5	5½	5⅞	6⅜	6⅞	7¼	7¾	8¼	8⅝	9⅛	9½
Aida 14	1⅜	1⅞	2⅛	2½	2⅞	3⅛	3½	3⅞	4¼	4⅝	5	5⅜	5¾	6	6⅜	6¾	7⅛	7½
Aida 18	1⅛	1⅜	1⅝	2	2¼	2½	2¾	3	3⅜	3⅝	3⅞	4¼	4½	4¾	5	5¼	5½	5⅞
100% Linen 18 (9 stitches per inch)	2⅛	2¾	3¼	3⅞	4⅜	5	5½	6⅛	6⅝	7⅛	7¾	8¼	8⅞	9⅜	10	10½	11⅛	11⅝
Hardanger 22	⅞	1⅛	1⅜	1⅝	1⅞	2⅛	2¼	2½	2¾	3	3⅛	3⅜	3⅝	3⅞	4⅛	4⅜	4½	4¾
Linen Plus 28 / 100% Linen 28 (14 stitches per inch)	1⅜	1⅞	2⅛	2½	2⅞	3⅛	3½	3⅞	4¼	4⅝	5	5⅜	5¾	6	6⅜	6¾	7⅛	7½
100% Linen 30 (15 stitches per inch)	1¼	1⅝	2	2¼	2⅝	3	3¼	3⅝	4	4¼	4⅝	5	5¼	5⅝	6	6¼	6⅝	7

STITCH COUNT FOR FABRIC	110	115	120	125	130	135	140	150	160	170	180	190	200	210	220	230	240	250
Herta 6	18⅜	19⅛	20	20⅞	21¾	22½	23⅜	25	26⅝	28⅜	30	31⅝	33⅜	35	36⅝	38⅜	40	41⅝
Aida 8	13¾	14⅜	15	15⅝	16¼	16⅞	17½	18¾	20	21¼	22½	23¾	25	26¼	27½	28¾	30	31¼
Aida 11	10	10½	10⅞	11⅜	11⅞	12¼	12¾	13⅝	14½	15½	16⅜	17¼	18¼	19⅛	20	21	21⅞	22¾
Aida 14	7⅞	8¼	8½	8⅞	9¼	9⅞	10	10¾	11½	12⅛	12⅞	13½	14¼	15	15¾	16⅜	17⅛	17⅞
Aida 18	6⅛	6⅜	6⅝	7	7¼	7½	7¾	8⅜	8⅞	9⅜	10	10½	11⅛	11⅝	12¼	12¾	13⅜	13⅞
100% Linen 18 (9 stitches per inch)	12⅛	12¾	13¼	13⅞	14⅜	15	15½	16⅝	17¾	18⅞	20	21⅛	22⅛	23¼	24⅜	25½	26⅝	27¾
Hardanger 22	5	5¼	5½	5⅜	5⅞	6⅛	6⅜	6⅞	7¼	7¾	8⅛	8⅝	9⅛	9½	10	10½	11	11⅜
Linen Plus 28 / 100% Linen 28 (14 stitches per inch)	7⅞	8¼	8½	8⅞	9¼	9⅞	10	10¾	11½	12⅛	12⅞	13½	14¼	15	15¾	16⅜	17⅛	17⅞
100% Linen 30 (15 stitches per inch)	7¼	7⅝	8	8¼	8⅝	9	9¼	10	10⅝	11¼	12	12⅝	13¼	14	14⅝	15¼	16	16⅝

Evenweave Computation Chart reprinted by special permission of Designs by Gloria & Pat, Inc. © 1986.

in Appendix I. Be sure to allow another two or three inches of unworked surface area to serve as a border or background and to be used in finishing.

Stitching With the Grain

Because no woven fabric is perfectly even, a convention has evolved of keeping the selvages on the right and left of the fabric to be stitched. This practice keeps stitching consistent from project to project and establishes a single count per piece of fabric (*see* Illustration 6).

Warp threads are vertical and weft (or woof) horizontal. If we know the vertical threads, we can determine where the selvages were. To figure out which threads are vertical, pull one out from each direction at the edge of the fabric. On close examination, one thread is wiggly and one straight—the wiggly thread is from the vertical direction and should be aligned top to bottom (*see* Illustration 7).

The smoother thread is a weft thread and so should run in a horizontal direction. (The conditions of weaving individual threads into fabric result in vertical threads being less straight.)

Marking the Top

Mark the top of your fabric in some way, to keep your project oriented correctly. (In stitching it may be necessary or desirable to turn your fabric upside down to complete an area.) Do not use pencil or ballpoint pen, which may rub off or run. Use a thread or permanent needlework marking pen. A vanishing needlework marking pen may make a mark that disappears prematurely, or worse, which cannot be erased because of an unknown chemical reaction (*see* Illustration 8).

Using a Hoop

Cross-stitch may be done with or without an embroidery hoop. When using a hoop, be sure to remove it after every stitching session, to prevent permanent hoop marks. Generally linen and linen-type fabrics are not worked on a hoop, while other fabrics are.

All Things

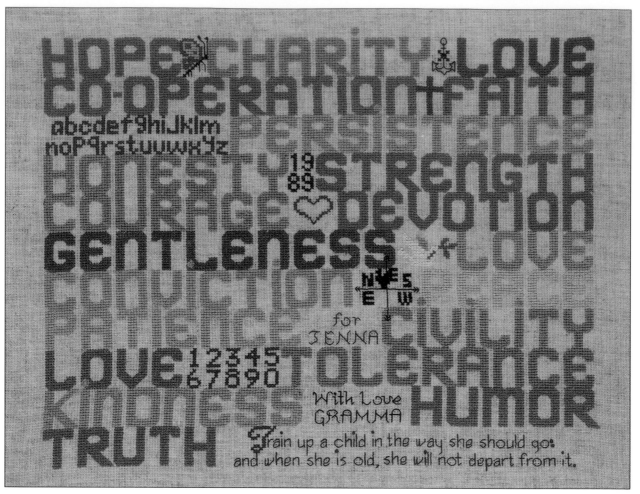

Train Up a Child

A House

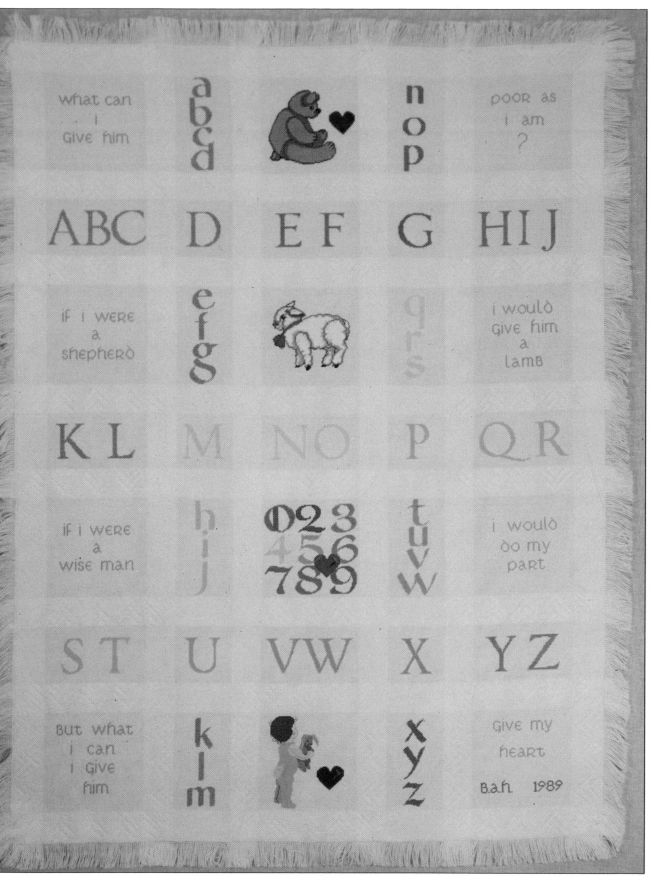

Baby Blanket

Little Lamb

Family Tree

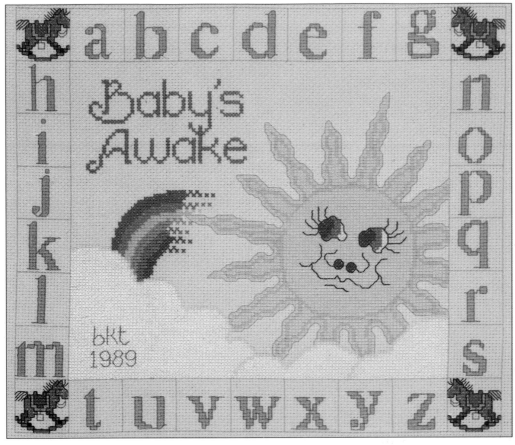

Baby's Awake

Baby's Asleep

A Babe in a House

Pippa Passes

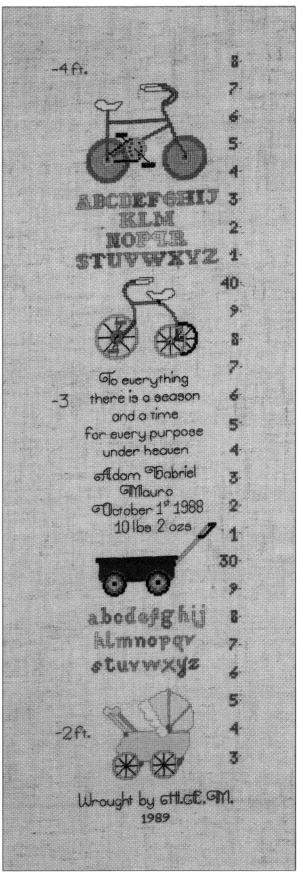

Growth Chart

Stitched by Me

Linen and Other Fabrics

You may distinguish linen (and linen types) by their lightly woven, rounded individual threads that cannot be easily pierced by a needle and that are distinctly separated from each other (*see* Illustration 9).

You may recognize other fabrics woven for cross-stitch by their tightly woven and interlocked surface, which resembles rows of boxes with tiny holes at each corner (*see* Illustration 10).

Cross-stitches make X's. On linen and linen types the X is made across an imagined box; on other fabrics each box (or square) can be seen and the holes at each corner provide a guide for the needle (*see* Illustrations 11 and 12).

Tapestry Needles

A blunt, or tapestry, needle should always be used for cross-stitch so that the fabric is not pierced or caught easily. The slightly rounded tip of a tapestry needle slides past the warp and weft threads of evenweave fabric and will not unexpectedly prick or catch the fabric (*see* Illustration 13).

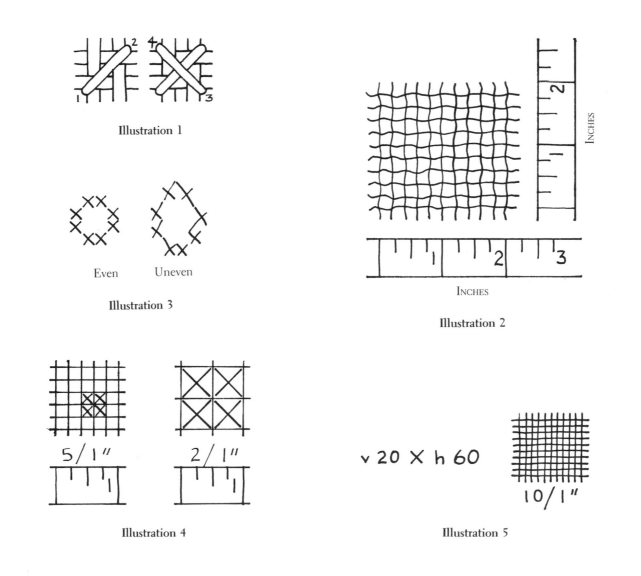

Illustration 1

Even   Uneven

Illustration 3

Illustration 2

5 / 1"   2 / 1"

Illustration 4

v 20 X h 60   10 / 1"

Illustration 5

Thread

Thread for cross-stitch is available in cotton, linen, wool, and metallics. Each fiber has its own characteristics of tension, finish, color range, thickness, and ease of handling. In our book we use and suggest various threads for each project, but one of the pleasures of counting from a graph is that the stitcher can change various elements (within a range), to render a unique finished design. At the back of this book we list and discuss various threads, including suggestions for sources. Most threads for cross-stitch are rather thin and are often used in multiple strands.

Number of Strands

To determine the number of strands to use, check our charts on page 19 or experiment with the fabric you have chosen. Avoid using so many strands that the fabric weave is crowded or distorted; by the same token, use enough to contrast the thickness of the stitch from that of the weave (*see* Illustration 14). Personally evaluate the finished effect. Some stitchers prefer a plump, rounded, filled-in finish, whereas others prefer a fine, delicate, airy look. The technique remains the same, and the ultimate decision of how many threads to use is yours.

Counted Cross-stitch

Our book presents counted cross-stitch charts. (Some cross-stitch designs are prestamped onto fabric, then covered as the surface is worked.) To stitch from a chart (or graph) keep the following rules in mind:

1. One square on the chart represents one stitch on the fabric. (Half stitches are represented by a diagonal line in the middle of the box, with either one or two smaller color symbols in the box) (*see* Illustration 15).

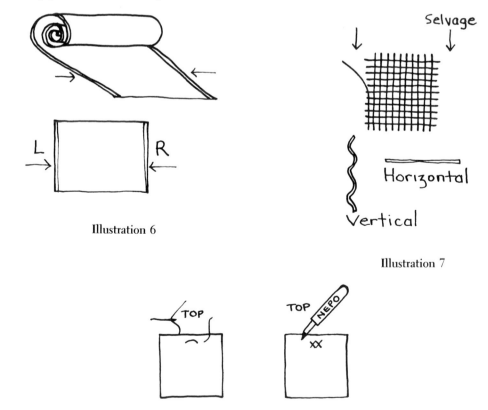

Illustration 6

Illustration 7

Illustration 8

Suggested Number of Thread
Strands for Cloth

	Aida				Loomspun	Ragusa	Rustico	
Cloth Count	11	14	18	22	14	14	14	18
Floss	3 or 4	3 or 2	2	1	2	1	2 or 3	1 or 2
Perle #5	1							
Medici	2	2	1	1	2	2	2	1
Blending Filament in Combination	1	1	1	1	1	1	1	1
Blending Filament Alone	3 or 4	3 or 4	2	2	3 or 4	3 or 4	3 or 4	2
Flower Thread	3	2	1	1	2	2	2	1

Suggested Number of Thread
Strands for Linen and Linenlike Cloths

Fiber Count	26	30	32	40
Floss	2	2	2	1
Blending Filament in Combination	1	1	1	1

2. A cross-stitch on fabric is an X made on a box or square on an evenweave fabric (*see* Illustration 1).
3. Each symbol represents a color (*see* Illustration 15).
4. Backstitches (used for definitions as in outlines) are indicated by solid lines between graphed symbols (*see* Illustration 16).
5. Backstitches are stitched after cross-stitches are completed and are stitched according to their placement on the graph (*see* Illustration 17).
6. Graphs are made on a grid of ten squares to the inch, and inches are marked with heavier lines. Graphs that are mechanically reproduced in printing will not measure ten stitches to the inch, but *represent* tens of stitches and remain proportionally correct (*see* Illustration 18).
7. Inch lines enable the stitcher to count large areas in tens (*see* Illustration 19).
8. To change borders or find additional numbers and letters for personalization, you will need to follow the directions in Appendix I.
9. Center lines or inch lines may be basted into the fabric to simplify counting squares or boxes on the fabric. These should be removed when the project is complete (*see* Illustrations 20 and 21).

Color Symbols

Each chart provides a color key that indicates what symbol represents what thread color. The type of thread used in the stitched sample will be indicated, but conversions to other yarns are encouraged.

To successfully alter colors or yarns, first look at all the original colors together with the fabric and then change colors or threads, being sure to retain color values, for contrast and loyalty to the original concept.

Stitch Progression

When stitching, complete colors in general areas before moving on, rather than haphazardly stitching color by color over the whole surface. Moving in a consistent direction after completing each color in an area will keep the surface even and make counting easier and more accurate. Establish a beginning point and

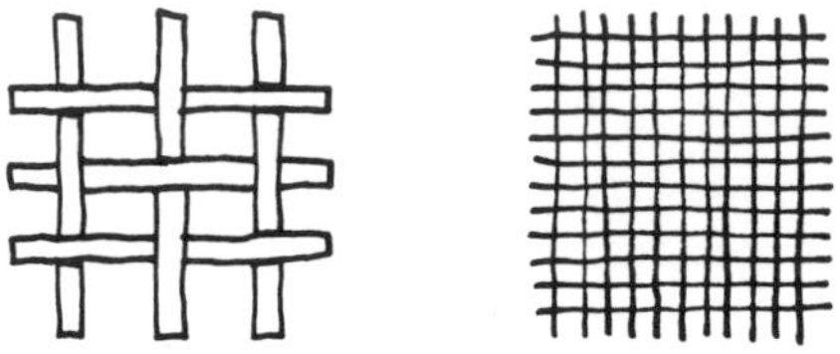

Linen

Illustration 9

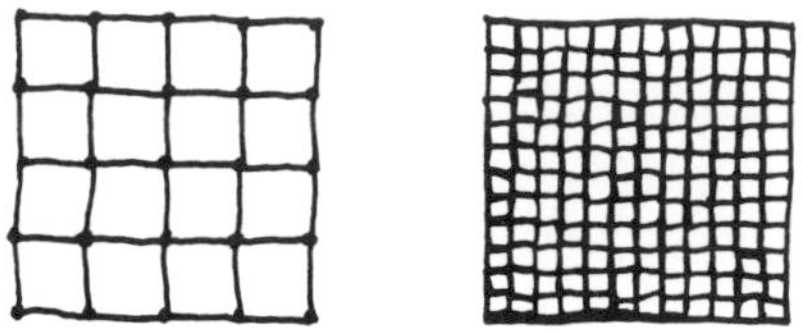

Aida,
Hardanger

Illustration 10

Cross-stitch on Aida

Illustration 11

Cross-stitch on Linen

Illustration 12

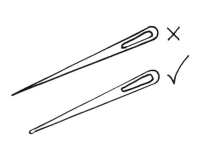

Illustration 13

Too Much
Thread

Too Little
Thread

Illustration 14

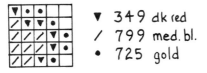

Illustration 15

Illustration 16

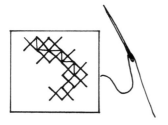

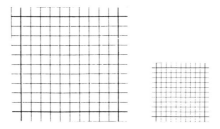

Illustration 17

Illustration 18

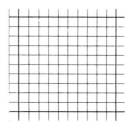

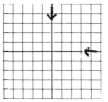

Illustration 19

Illustration 20

develop the work from there. We usually recommend beginning in the center of the chart and the center of the fabric (*see* Illustration 22). This will insure that the pattern does not run too close to the edge of the cut fabric or at worst run right off the edge (*see* Illustration 23).

Finding the Center

To find the center of a piece of fabric, fold it in half both ways and crease it. Mark the middle with a pin or thread. The center of each chart is indicated by small arrows at the top or bottom and one side. When choosing not to work from the center, count very, very carefully to the starting point and mark it. Then count again, on fabric and chart.

Beginning to Stitch

Each cross-stitch consists of a bottom stroke of the needle and thread, slanting from lower left to upper right, and a second stroke that lies on top, slanting from lower right to upper left, across a square or box in the fabric (*see* Illustration 24). Begin each row at the left, working across the row (counting symbols on the chart) toward the right to lay the first half of the stitch (*see* Illustration 25). At the end of the row, bring the needle up at the lower right and down (stitching across the laid thread) at the upper left to complete the X. Continue toward the left of the row. Progress to the next row *below* the initial row (*see* Illustration 26).

Cross-stitch should always be worked downward from the starting point. By working the stitches as described, the stitcher will create only horizontal and vertical threads on the back of the fabric. This method prevents distortion and saves thread; slanting stitches on the back pull the weave and take up more thread, because they are longer (*see* Illustration 27). When stitching on linen, begin the first stitch by bringing the needle up next to an intersection of fabric threads that has the warp (vertical) thread on top (*see* Illustration 28). This will prevent the stitching thread from slipping under the weave of the fabric, and because the fabric threads will always be covered in twos, all stitches in the project will then begin at a corner with a vertical thread. If there are not enough stitches together to make a horizontal row, stitch each X at a time, making the top stroke as soon as the bottom stroke is completed, and progress to the next stitch underneath or underneath and to one side.

If a color area cannot be stitched properly in a downward direction, turn the fabric (and the chart!) upside down and work as described. This will insure that stitches do not slant on the back. Once in a while a slanted stitch on the back of the fabric is inevitable, but in general it should be avoided, and if in following a color one needs to make a series of stitches incorrectly, be sure to rotate the design 180° (upside down).

Waste Knots

Do not make knots, either in stopping or starting, but rather work threads into already established areas (*see* Illustration 29). If you have no stitches to "bury" your thread into (pierce the existing stitch threads), use a waste knot that will hold a piece of thread taut until you have completed your strand and then rethread the knotted piece, and bury the tail (*see* Illustration 30).

To make a waste knot, push the needle down from the front of the fabric, threaded with a knotted strand some distance (two or three inches) above the starting point. The knot will hold the thread until you are ready to cut it off. Rethread the "tail" and "bury" it. (Once again, be sure to pierce the worked stitches on the back so that the tail will not slip.) Cut it off with *no ends* dangling, so you will not see a shadow from the front. The lack of dangling ends will also prevent tangles and unintended knots.

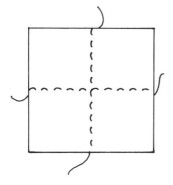

Illustration 21

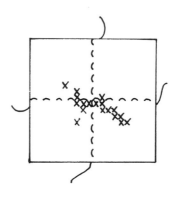

Illustration 22

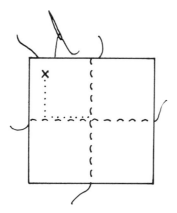

Illustration 23

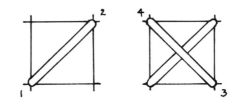

Illustration 24

Illustration 25

Illustration 26

Stitching Aids

Some stitchers like to mark the completed stitches on the chart. Do this with a transparent (light yellow or aqua) felt pen so that the symbols can still be seen in case anything needs to be reworked or you decide to stitch the design again.

Many other products are available to enhance stitching, including magnifying accessories, frames (to hold the hoop), lights, magnetic boards, and locating magnetic bars (to underline the row being worked), magnetic needle holders, and of course systems for storing and sorting threads and charts. Before investing in accessories, stitch at least one design so that you will develop a sense of what you will need.

Before You Start

Remember: Before you start stitching, be sure your fabric is big enough. Use the stitch computation chart on page 16 to find out how big the design will be on your fabric, keeping in mind that you need to halve the count for linen and linenlike fabrics, then add two or three inches for background, border, and finishing. Find the middle of your chart and your fabric. Then count—carefully! Above all, enjoy the fascinating process of seeing the design emerge, stitch by stitch, from your blank surface.

Washing

When the project is completed, you may wash it before having it framed or otherwise finished, but be sure to set the colors first by immersing the whole piece of fabric in a basin of cold water, salt, and white vinegar (proportions for one gallon of water are two teaspoons of salt and a half cup of white vinegar). Let the piece soak for twenty minutes or so, gently pushing it from side to side at least once. Then rinse it in cold water for five to ten minutes. Wash it in cold water and a mild soap (such as Ivory), without agitating. Then rinse again several times, or soak the piece for ten to fifteen minutes. Let it drain, place it between layers of clean, white toweling (not patterned paper towels—the pattern may bleed!), and roll, squeezing gently. Unwrap the project and place it facedown on clean, white toweling, then press under a clean, thin, white fabric. Do not steam the piece, as its dampness is sufficient (with the heat of the iron) to smooth out any creases. As the piece is ironed it will dry, perhaps completely. If not, leave it overnight.

Mounting

Cross-stitch should be framed or mounted with acid-free materials, so that the chemical composition of the natural fibers is not threatened.

As to using glass or not, that is a subjective decision to be made with the following understanding: glass will protect your piece—from smoke, fingers, pen tips, and other inadvertent threats. On the other hand, glass removes the immediacy and tactility of stitched work and may be aesthetically unsettling. If you use glass, mount it so that it does not touch the surface of the work. Nonglare glass should *not* be used, as it tends to make what it covers look fuzzy when it cannot rest directly on it. Nonglare glass may also threaten fibers, because of its composition and the effect it has on light.

Also be sure to view your piece against a light surface and a dark one. Depending on the fabric, the threads used, and the tension of the stitches, the underlying color on which you mount your piece will distinctly influence the finished look.

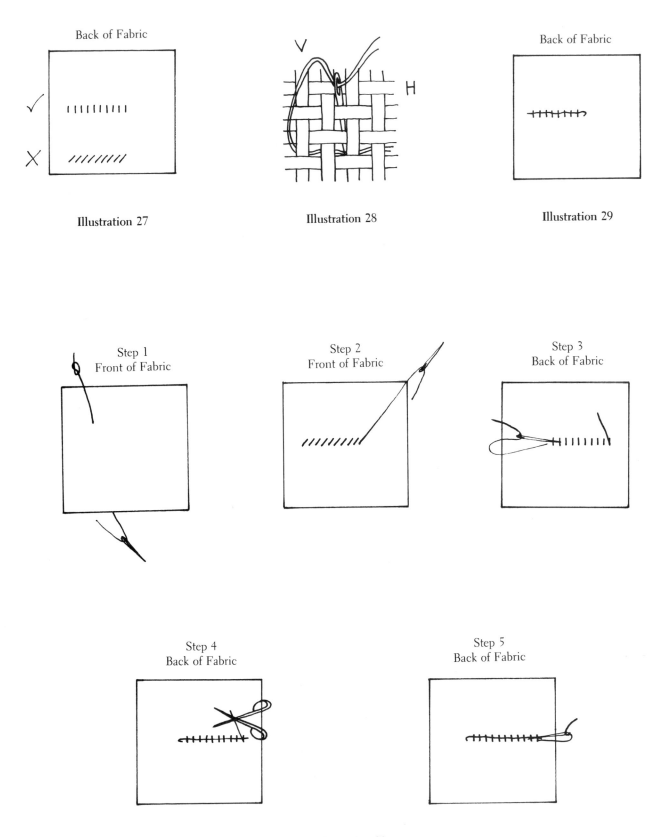

Back of Fabric

Illustration 27

Illustration 28

Back of Fabric

Illustration 29

Step 1
Front of Fabric

Step 2
Front of Fabric

Step 3
Back of Fabric

Step 4
Back of Fabric

Step 5
Back of Fabric

Illustration 30

Pillows and Linens

For pillows and linens, be sure to use cotton, linen, or wool threads and fabrics in finishing. Do not use spray or protective chemical coatings. These may destroy the fibers over time and may discolor the surface.

Mistakes

Finally, as a reassuring note, do not despair if your count is slightly off. By compensating for or overlooking insignificant errors, you can enjoy a piece that may not perfectly match the chart. On the other hand, check your count frequently, for errors in one color will affect the placement of every other stitch. Ripping, or "unstitching" should be thought of as an integral part of counting cross-stitch, and everybody does it from time to time.

2
Samplers for the Nursery

Samplers for the nursery are a special joy to stitch, whether in preparation for the birth of a baby or as a present for one who has already arrived. By including the baby's name, birth date, height, and weight, you will make a unique treasure. Taking the time and care to use good materials and meticulous technique will provide the family with a timeless document that brings pleasure for years to come.

When choosing or designing a sampler for the nursery, consider the following choices. You may stitch a design that:

> Matches elements in the room (wallpaper, quilt, sheets, or artwork)
> Matches the room's colors
> Complements the colors and decor
> Stands alone

Very few charts are available that exactly match fabric or wallpaper, but that does not mean a sampler cannot look very much like the nursery's decor. Find animals or shapes, numbers or letters, that look similar to those being used and coordinate the suggested floss colors to match. Or you may decide to simply match colors from the nursery in a sampler that does not include designs from the decor. Using swatches of paint, wallpaper, or fabric, alter the colors indicated in the pattern you would like to use. (You may need help in a yarn store, from those accustomed to changing colors.) To retain the impact of the original color scheme, be sure to retain the values, paying attention to contrast and line. First pull all the recommended colors. Then, with help if necessary, select the coordinating colors. By stitching the sampler in colors you have chosen, you will achieve a pleasing, coordinated effect, even if the pattern itself does not incorporate designs from the decor.

Perhaps you will choose a design that complements the feeling of the decor in the nursery, rather than matching the design elements or exact colors. For example, a boldly colored contemporary pattern will be a special highlight in a nursery filled with primary colors or simple geometric shapes. Or a reproduction of an early American sampler will beautifully enhance a baby's room filled with traditional furniture and muted colors.

The delight of a design that stands alone resides in its timeless quality. When considering such a pattern, the stitcher need only select a sampler that will be a joy to stitch and to give, however simple or oft repeated. As with favorite baby-blanket patterns or smocked gowns, some samplers for the nursery are stitched over and over again, changed only by the addition of a unique name and birth date.

All things bright and beautiful,
All creatures great and small,
All things wise and wonderful,
The Lord God made them all.

All Things

SYMBOL	COLOR	DMC #
+	ANTIQUE BLUE – DARK	930
*	SHELL PINK – DARK	221
•	STEEL GREY – DARK	414
▲	PEWTER GREY – DARK	413
X	SHELL PINK – MEDIUM	223
O	SHELL PINK – LIGHT	224
I	SHELL PINK – V. LIGHT	225
V	ANTIQUE BLUE – MEDIUM	931
L	ANTIQUE BLUE – LIGHT	932
=	SPORTSMAN FLESH – MEDIUM	3064
S	NEGRO FLESH	632
–	GREEN GREY	3053
■	GREEN GREY – DARK	3051
#	BROWN GREY – DARK	3021
Q	BEIGE GREY – V. DARK	640
↑	HAZELNUT BROWN – DARK	420
∩	OLD GOLD – LIGHT	676
\	YELLOW – LIGHT PALE	745
·	WHITE	BLANC
··	BEIGE BROWN	840
/	PEACH FLESH – LIGHT	754

BACKSTITCH VERSE IN #221

A Babe in a House

SYMBOL	COLOR	DMC#
■	AQUAMARINE – MEDIUM	943
✳	SEAGREEN – DARK	958
S	SEAGREEN – MEDIUM	959
\	SEAGREEN – LIGHT	964
–	ROYAL BLUE	797
▼	DELFT – DARK	798
•	DELFT – MEDIUM	799
✳	BLUE VIOLET – DARK	333

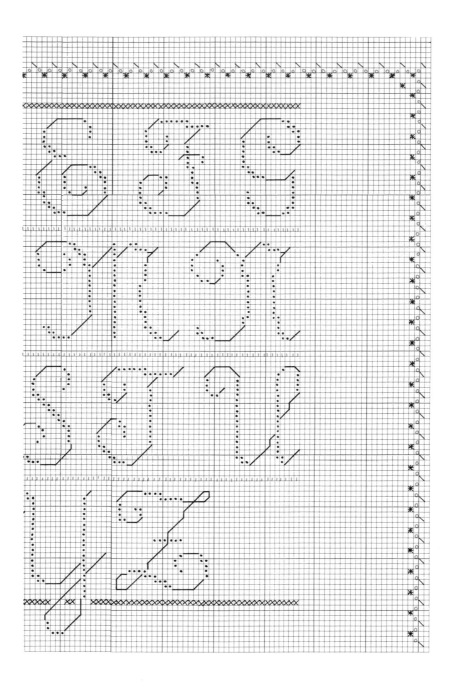

×	BLUE VIOLET – MEDIUM	340
I	BLUE VIOLET – LIGHT	341
o	PLUM – V. LIGHT	3608
+	PLUM – ULTRA LIGHT	3609
··	OFF WHITE	746
n	YELLOW – LT. PALE	745
▲	BEIGE BROWN – V. DARK	838
ᖉ	BEIGE BROWN – LIGHT	841

A babe i
is a u
of

=	SPORTSMAN FLESH	945
.	WHITE	BLANC
V	TERRA COTTA – LIGHT	758
9	SPORTSMAN FLESH – LIGHT	950
z	PEACH FLESH – LIGHT	754

n a house
ellspring
pleasure.
anon. 1838

Joshua
Abraham
Zadikoff

June 15, 1985
6 lbs 3 oz
19 3/4 in

W	PEACH FLESH – V. LIGHT	948
L	BEIGE BROWN – V. LIGHT	842
II	BEIGE BROWN – ULTRA V. LIGHT	543
U	BABY PINK	818
↑	BABY PINK – LIGHT	819

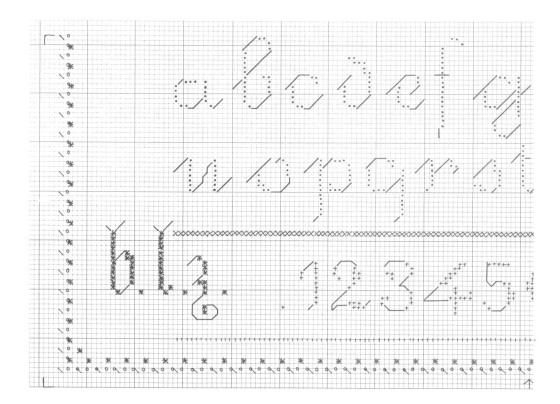

BACKSTITCH ON: UPPER CASE LETTERING #799

VERSE, BABY'S NAME, BIRTHDATE, ETC. #797

BLACK BACKSTITCH LINES ON DECORATIVE SIDES #798

GREEN BACKSTITCH LINES ON DECORATIVE SIDES #959

BLACK BACKSTITCH LINES ON FRAME #340

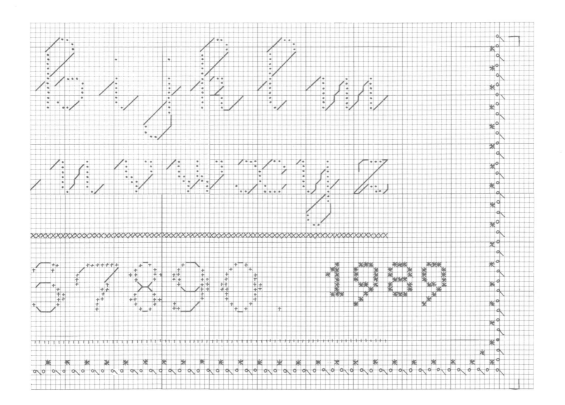

GREEN BACKSTITCH LINES ON FRAME #943

BACKSTITCH ON LOWER CASE LETTERING #799

BACKSTITCH ON STITCHERS INITIALS #333

BACKSTITCH BEWEEN MOTHER & BABY #841

BACKSTITCH ON NUMERALS #3609

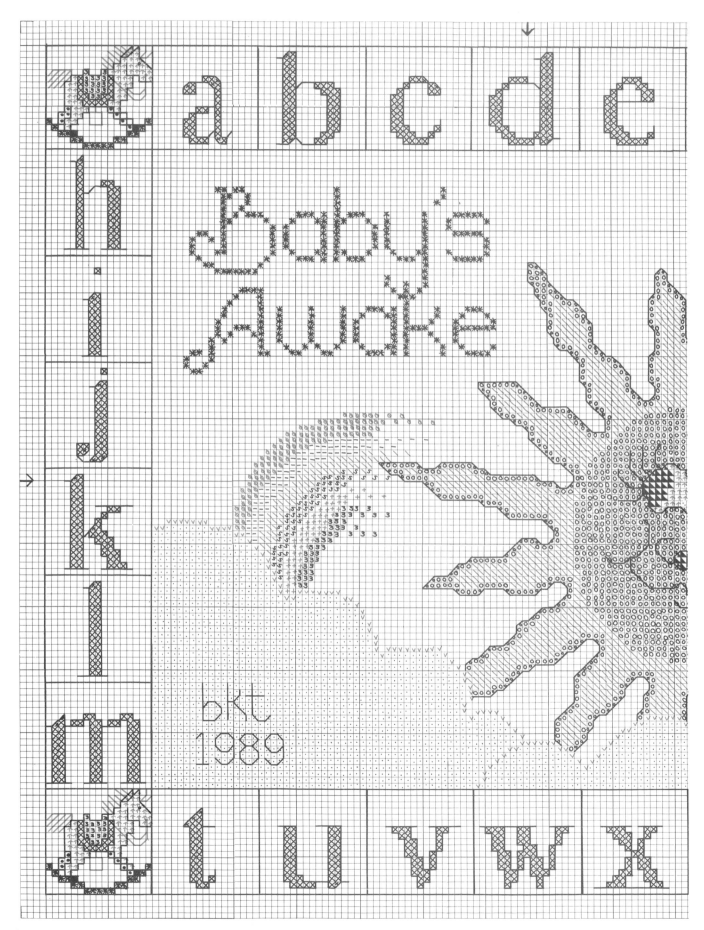

Baby's Awake

bkt
1989

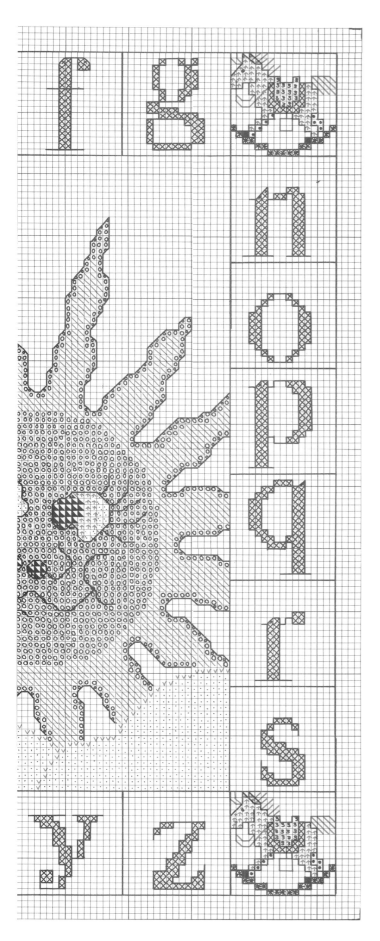

Baby's Awake

SYMBOL	COLOR	DMC FLOSS #
X	SEA GREEN – MEDIUM	959
*	AQUAMARINE – MEDIUM	943
\	YELLOW – MEDIUM	743
O	YELLOW – PALE	744
∴	OFF WHITE	746
▶	COFFEE BROWN – DARK	801
■	BLACK BROWN	3371
V	SKY BLUE – V. LIGHT	747
·	WHITE	BLANC
⊘	PLUM – LIGHT	3607
–	APRICOT – MEDIUM	3340
S	NILE GREEN – MEDIUM	913
+	WEDGEWOOD – LIGHT	518
3	LAVENDER – V. DARK	208
•	BROWN – MEDIUM	433
B'ST	CANARY – DEEP	972

BACKSTITCH BETWEEN & AROUND ALPHABET – # 959

BACKSTITCH ON ALPHABET, INITIALS, REINS & STIRRUP ON ROCKING HORSE – # 943

BACKSTITCH AROUND SUN – # 972

BACKSTITCH ROCKING HORSE MANE & TAIL – # 801

BACKSTITCH ON SUN FACE & ALL REMAINING BACKSTITCH ON ROCKING HORSE – # 3371

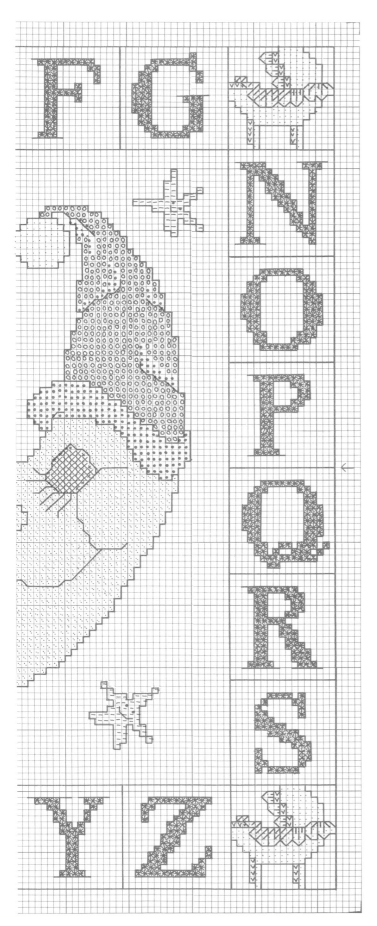

Baby's Asleep

SYMBOL	COLOR	DMC FLOSS #
\	SEA GREEN – MEDIUM	959
*	AQUAMARINE – MEDIUM	943
∴	OFF WHITE	746
•	WEDGEWOOD – LIGHT	518
o	SKY BLUE	519
×	YELLOW – LIGHT PALE	745
–	WHITE WITH ONE STRAND BALGER BLENDING FILAMENT "VATICAN GOLD"	BLANC/BALGER #102C
v	SKY BLUE – VERY LIGHT	747
	WHITE	BLANC
B'ST	WEDGEWOOD – MEDIUM	517
B'ST	LAVENDER – DARK	209
B'ST	SEA GREEN – DARK	958
B'ST	TANGERINE – LIGHT	742
B'ST	GOLDEN BROWN – MEDIUM	976

BACKSTITCH BETWEEN & AROUND ALPHABET – #943

BACKSTITCH ON ALPHABET & INITIALS – #959

BACKSTITCH ON HAT – #517

BACKSTITCH AROUND MOON – #742

BACKSTITCH MOON FEATURES – #976

BACKSTITCH ON BASSINET – #518

BACKSTITCH BLACK OUTLINE & FEATURES ON STARS – #209

BACKSTITCH GREEN OUTLINE & FEATURES ON STARS – #958

WHEN USING 14 COUNT FABRIC, USE TWO THREADS TO BACKSTITCH.

Joshua Martin Hemberger
July 4, 1985
weight: 6 pounds
length: 19 inches

A House

SYMBOL	COLOR	DMC#
X	YELLOW – DARK	444
O	YELLOW – MEDIUM	307
·	YELLOW – LIGHT	445
S	RED – DARK	304
\	RED – MEDIUM	891
–	RED – LIGHT	3706
Q	BLUE – DARK	796
↑	BLUE – MEDIUM	798
+	BLUE – LIGHT	809
●	GREEN – DARK	699
V	GREEN – MEDIUM	701
I	GREEN – LIGHT	703
B'ST	BLACK	310

ALL BACKSTITCHING IN #310.

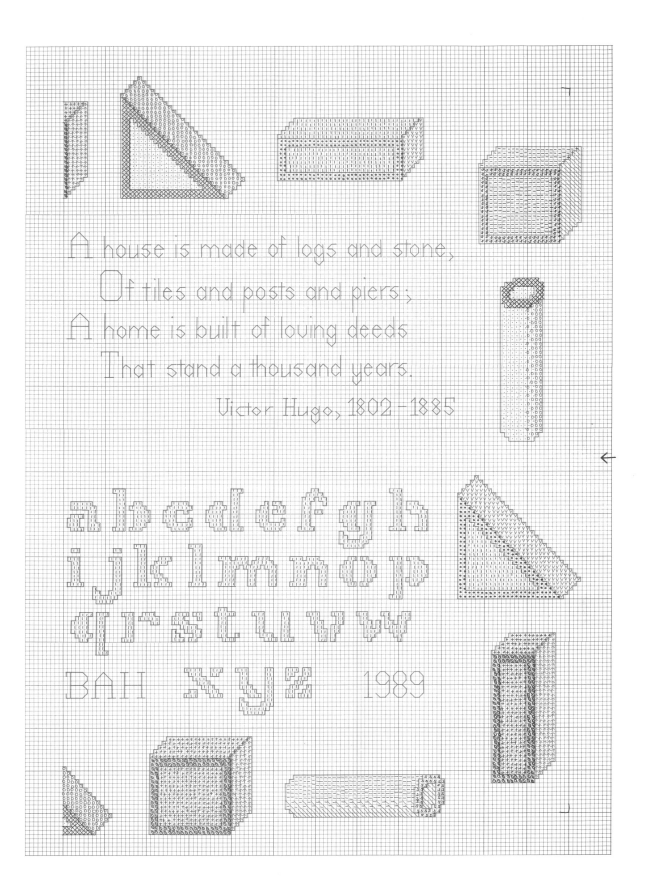

A house is made of logs and stone,
Of tiles and posts and piers;
A home is built of loving deeds
That stand a thousand years.
Victor Hugo, 1802-1885

abcdefgh
ijklmnop
qrstuvw
BAH xyz 1989

Baby Blanket

SYMBOL	COLOR	DMC FLOSS #	SYMBOL	COLOR	DMC FLOSS #
X	SEAGREEN – MED.	959	Z	SEAGREEN – DARK	958
O	LAVENDER – MED.	210	T	WEDGEWOOD – LIGHT	518
●	LAVENDER – DARK	209	d	PLUM – LIGHT	3607
\	PLUM – ULTRA LIGHT	3609	F	TOPAZ – DARK	781
–	CRANBERRY – LIGHT	604	8	CHRISTMAS GOLD	783
3	CARNATION – V. LIGHT	894	∴	SPORTSMAN FLESH – V. LT	951
·	TAN – LIGHT	437	↑	SEAGREEN – LIGHT	964
Q	BROWN – V. LIGHT	435	⁚	SKY BLUE – V. LIGHT	747
=	BROWN – MED.	433	U	BROWN GREY – LIGHT	3023
▲	COFFEE BROWN – ULTRA DARK	938	II	BROWN GREY – MEDIUM	3022
◼	BLACK	310	//	BROWN GREY – V. LIGHT	3024
✳	BLACK BROWN	3371	A	BROWN GREY – DARK	3021
/	OFF WHITE	746		TAN	436
E	ROSE – VERY DEEP	326	✶	SHELL PINK – MED.	223
N	CARNATION – MED.	892	W	SHELL PINK – DARK	221
#	CARNATION – DARK	893	e	SHELL PINK – LIGHT	224
I	APRICOT	3341	J	AQUAMARINE – MEDIUM	943
+	YELLOW – PALE	744	4	NILE GREEN – LIGHT	955
S	LEMON – LIGHT	445	▲	NILE GREEN	954
6	AVOCADO GREEN – ULTRA LIGHT	472	∩	SKY BLUE	519
··	WHITE	BLANC	b	BLUE VIOLET – LIGHT	341
L	PEARL GREY	415	K	BLUE VIOLET – MEDIUM	340
◣	STEEL GREY – DARK	414	H	PLUM – V. LIGHT	3608
Y	PEWTER GREY – DARK	413			
7	PEARL GREY – V. LIGHT	762			
5	TERRA COTTA – MEDIUM	356			
◤	TERRA COTTA – LIGHT	758			
Δ	MAHOGANY – MEDIUM	301			
V	MAHOGANY – V. DARK	300			
2	GOLDEN BROWN – LIGHT	977			

BACKSTITCH INSTRUCTIONS:
BABY'S HAIR — 433
BUNNY — 3021
BABY'S FACE — 436

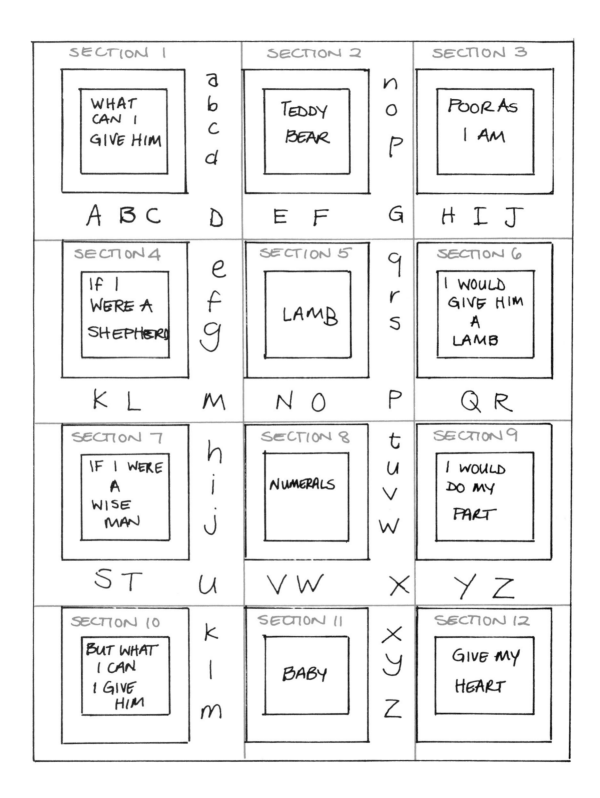

SECTION 1

WHAT CAN I GIVE HIM

a b c d

A B C D

SECTION 2

TEDDY BEAR

n o P

E F G

SECTION 3

POOR AS I AM

H I J

SECTION 4

If I WERE A SHEPHERD

e f g

K L M

SECTION 5

LAMB

q r s

N O P

SECTION 6

I WOULD GIVE HIM A LAMB

Q R

SECTION 7

IF I WERE A WISE MAN

h i j

S T U

SECTION 8

NUMERALS

t u v w

V W X

SECTION 9

I WOULD DO MY PART

Y Z

SECTION 10

BUT WHAT I CAN I GIVE HIM

k l m

SECTION 11

BABY

x y z

SECTION 12

GIVE MY HEART

what can
I
Give him

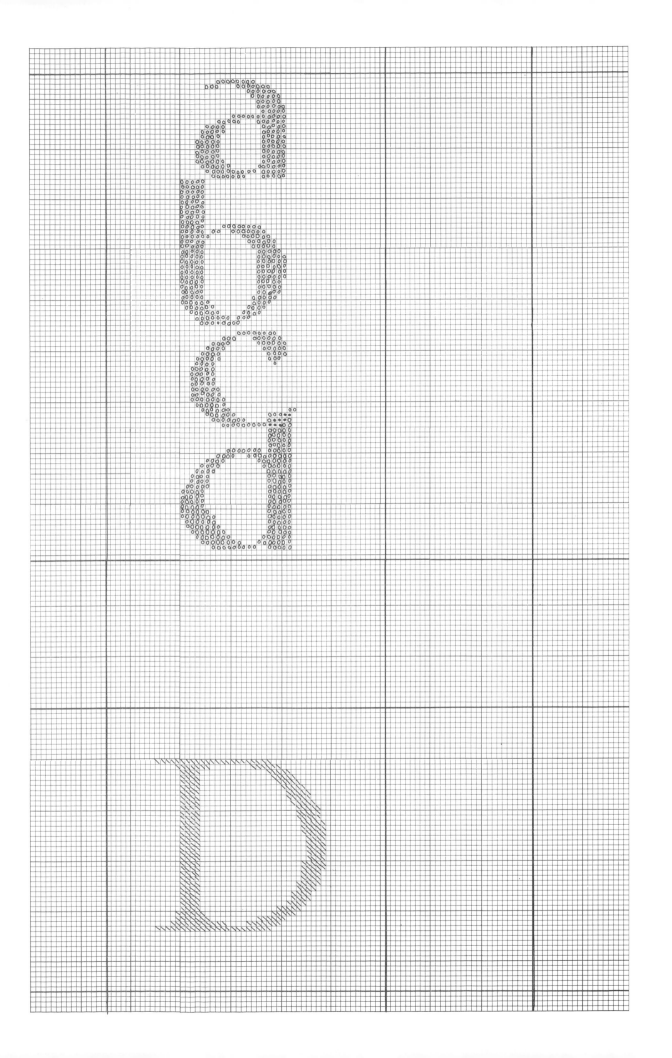

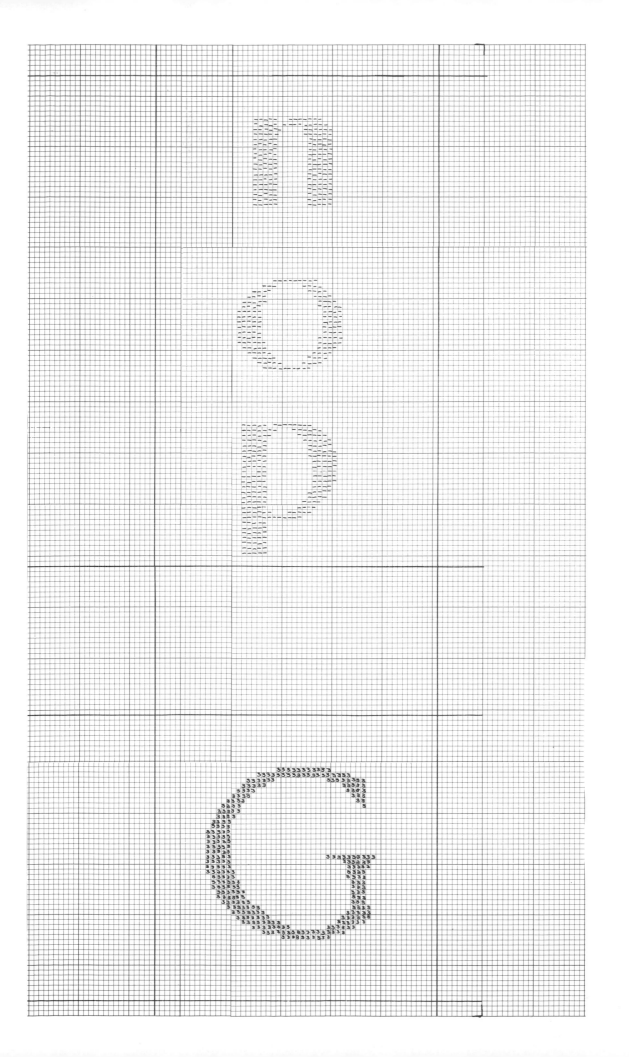

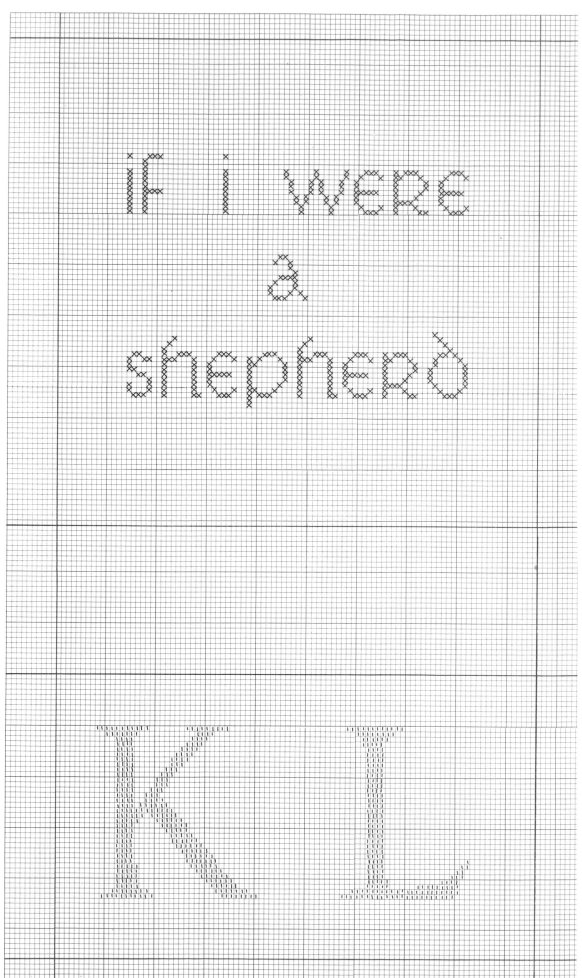

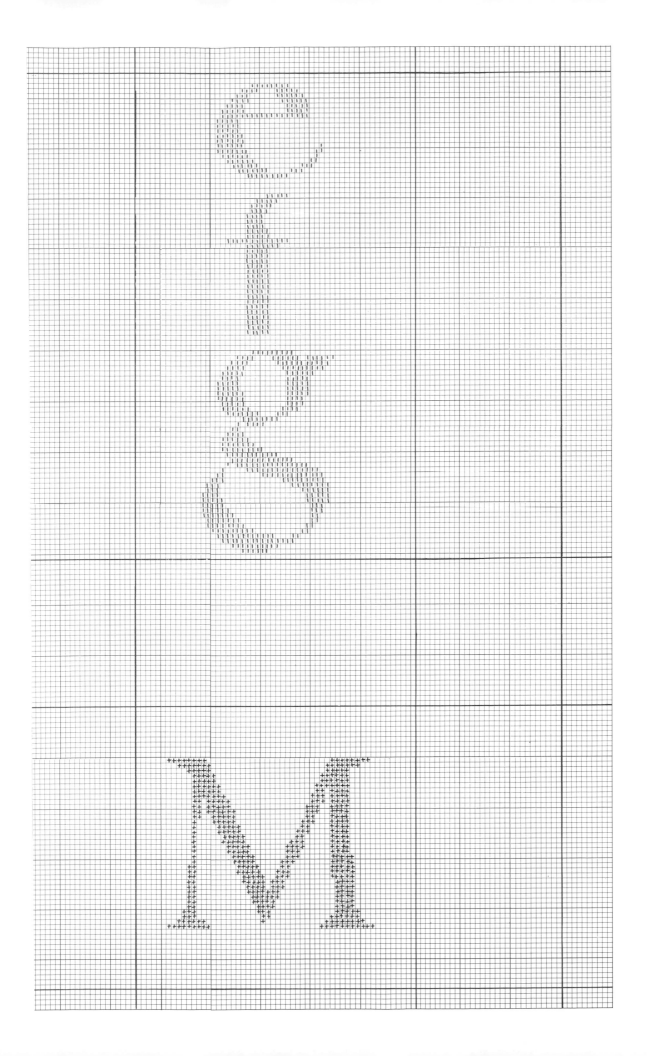

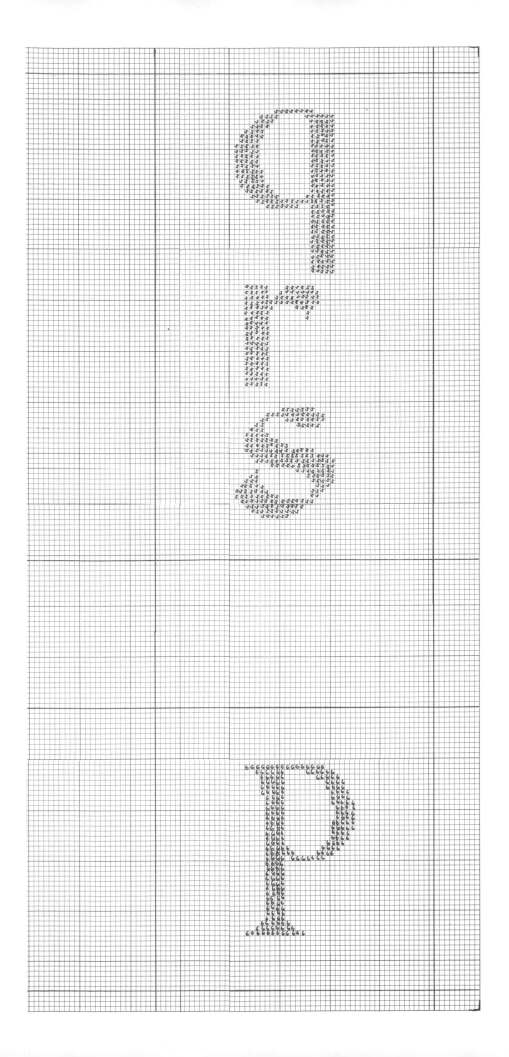

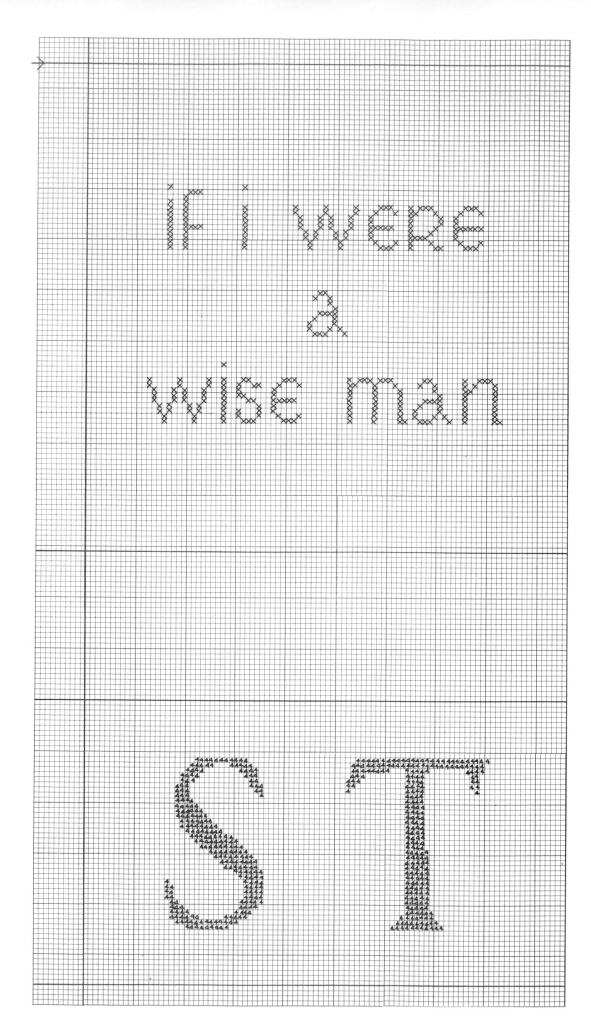

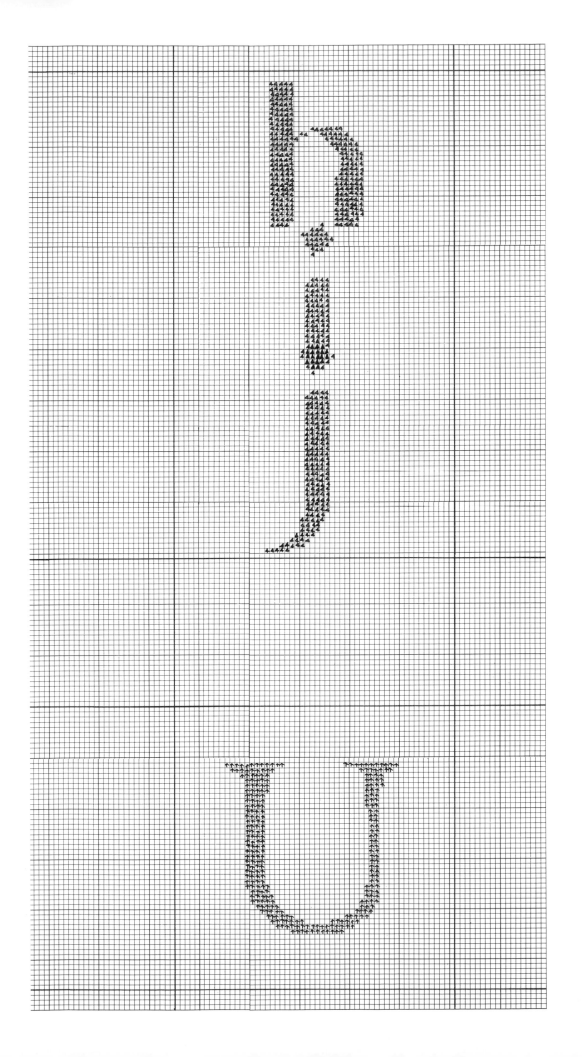

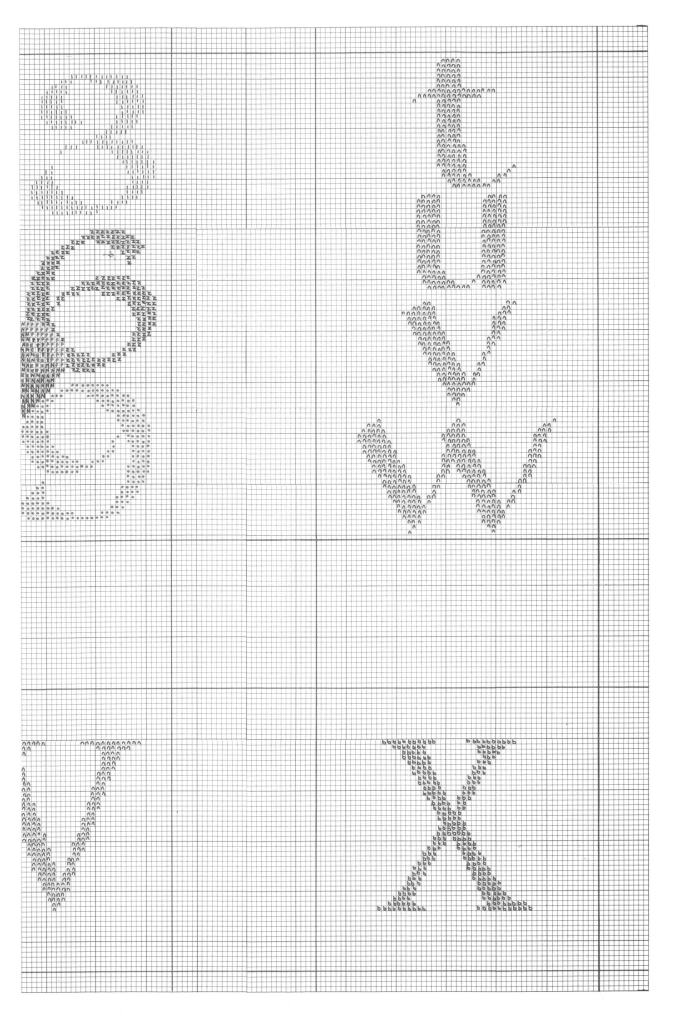

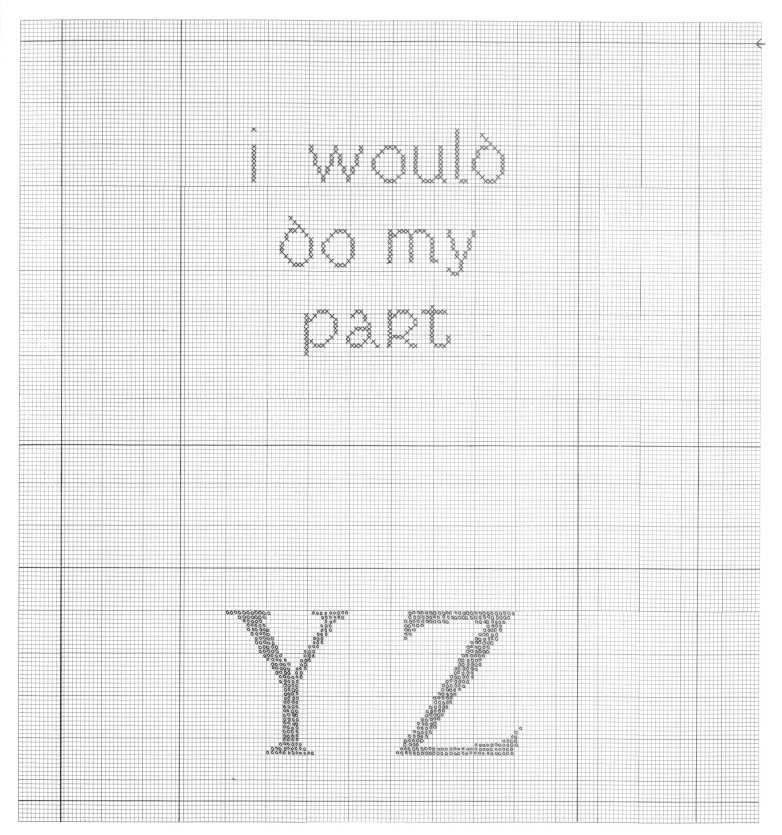

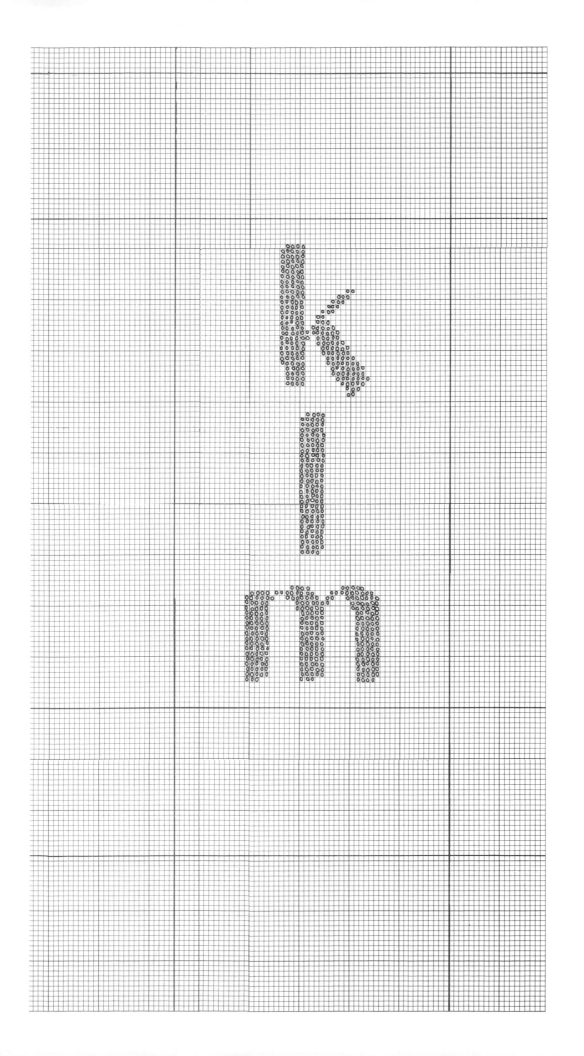

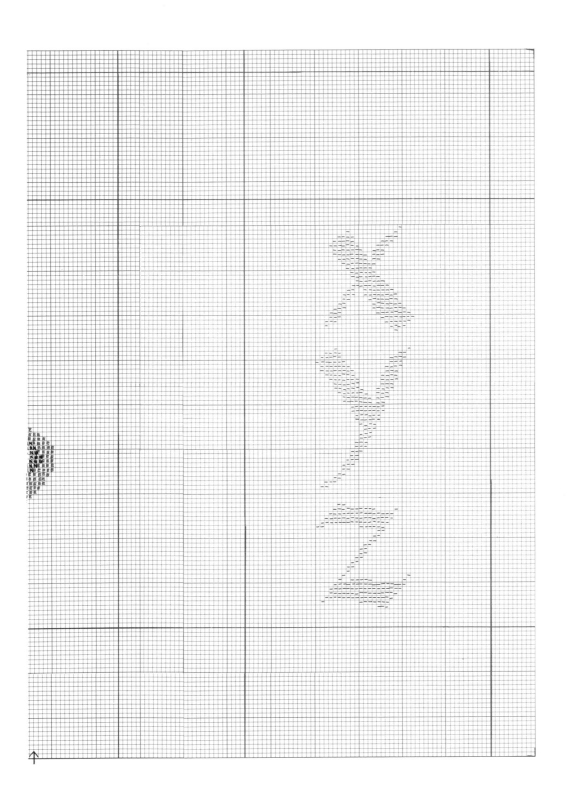

3
Samplers for Children's Rooms

As in any needlework project, when choosing a design for a child's room, decide whether the piece will stand on its own, match, or complement the decor of the room (*see* Chapter 2). Consider, too, how the piece will be finished—in a frame, as a pillow, a growth chart, in a mirror, tray, or box. While a birth date may be included in the design, usually height and weight at birth are not included in children's samplers. But the town or city, county, or country of residence may be. (This can be especially fun for children learning about geography.) Including the child's name makes the sampler really meaningful, and your initials and date contribute to the feeling that the project was done by a favorite grown-up for a special child.

Pippa Passes

SYMBOL	COLOR	DMC FLOSS #
ALGERIAN EYE STITCH	COPPER — SHADED	69
·	WHITE	BLANC
■	BLACK	310
∩	DUSTY ROSE — V. LIGHT	963
I	DUSTY ROSE — LIGHT	3354
＼	DUSTY ROSE — MEDIUM	962
∴	PEACH FLESH — V. LIGHT	948
—	PEACH FLESH — LIGHT	754
•	TERRA COTTA — LIGHT	758
L	MOCHA BROWN — V. LIGHT	3033
⊗	MOCHA BROWN — MEDIUM	3052
◣	MOCHA BROWN — V. DARK	3031
#	BEAVER GREY — ULTRA DARK	844
=	OLD GOLD — V. LIGHT	677
/	OLD GOLD — LIGHT	676
3	OLD GOLD — DARK	680
8	DRAB BROWN — DARK	611
U	AVOCADO GREEN — ULTRA LIGHT	472
Y	AVOCADO GREEN — V. LIGHT	471
▲	AVOCADO GREEN — LIGHT	470
O	BLUE VIOLET — LIGHT	341
+	BLUE VIOLET — MEDIUM	340
✳	BLUE VIOLET — DARK	333
◤	STEEL GREY — LIGHT	318
Z	PEWTER GREY	317
↑	BEIGE BROWN — LIGHT	841
Δ	HAZEL NUT BROWN — V. LIGHT	869
X	BEIGE BROWN — DARK	839
E	TOPAZ — V. LIGHT	727
S	TOPAZ — LIGHT	726
V	PEACH FLESH	353
⊙	CORAL — LIGHT	352
M	CORAL	351
N	PLUM — ULTRA LIGHT	3609
2	PLUM — V. LIGHT	3608
II	PLUM — LIGHT	3607
K	LAVENDER — MEDIUM	210
J	LAVENDER — DARK	209
W	LAVENDER — V. DARK	208
＼	BLUE — SHADED	124

ALL BACKSTITCHING — #333

ABCDEFG
HIJKLMN
OPQRSTU
VWXYZ

Shannon Elizabeth   October 5
Self   1977

The larks on the wing;
The snails on the thorn;
God's in his heaven—
All's right with the world!
ROBERT BROWNING
FROM "PIPPA PASSES"

abcdefghi
jklmmnopq
rstuvwxy
z
1234567 89
0
Stitched by Grammy   October 1989

Little lamb
who made thee ?
Dost thou know who made thee ?

for Adam on his birthday   Wrought k

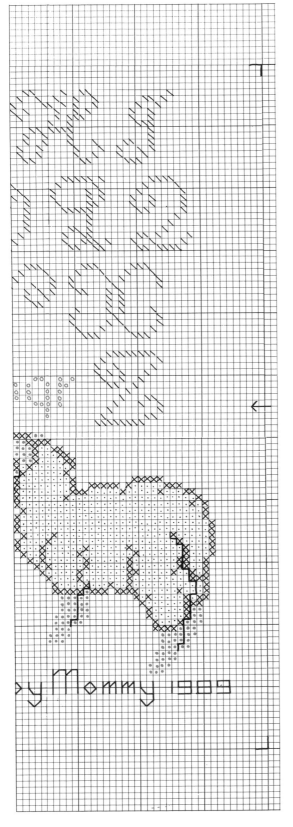

Little Lamb

SYMBOL	COLOR	EVA ROSENSTAND DANISH FLOWER THREAD #
\	BLUE-GREEN	197
×	BEAVER GREY	136
o	PINK	119
•	BLACK	240
.	CREAM	02

ALL BACKSTITCHING IN BLACK

Train Up a Child

SYMBOL	COLOR	DMC #
X	ANTIQUE MAUVE – MEDIUM	316
⋊	OLD GOLD – LIGHT	676
◢	BLACK	310
6	SALMON – DARK	347
–	BLUE GREEN – MEDIUM	503
O	ANTIQUE VIOLET – MEDIUM	3041
I	SPORTSMAN FLESH – MEDIUM	3064
\	BEAVER GREY – MEDIUM	647
•	SHELL PINK – DARK	221
+	SHELL PINK – LIGHT	224
V	GREY GREEN – MEDIUM	927
■	BLUE GREEN – V. DARK	500
↑	SHELL PINK – MEDIUM	223
∩	SKY BLUE	519
·	WHITE	BLANC
S	JADE – MEDIUM	562
Q	SHELL PINK – V. LIGHT	225
L	ANTIQUE MAUVE – LIGHT	778
#	OLD GOLD – V. LIGHT	677
✻	PEACH FLESH	353
U	ANTIQUE VIOLET – LIGHT	3042
//	MOCHA BROWN – MEDIUM	3032
∴	ANTIQUE BLUE – LIGHT	932

BACKSTITCH ON ANCHOR #310
BACKSTITCH ON BUTTERFLY #310
BACKSTITCH "FOR JENNA" #3687
BACKSTITCH "WITH LOVE GRAMMA #500
BACKSTITCH ON WEATHER VANE #310
BACKSTITCH "TRAIN UP..." #221

Growth Chart

SYMBOL	COLOR	DMC #
X	JADE – V. DARK	561
O	YELLOW – PALE	744
↑	SHELL GREY – LIGHT	453
•	SHELL GREY – DARK	451
\	TOPAZ	725
·	YELLOW – LT. PALE	745
ı	OFF WHITE	746
▶	BLACK	310
+	SALMON – DARK	347
Q	SALMON – MEDIUM	3328
#	CORNFLOWER BLUE – DARK	792
—	CORNFLOWER BLUE – MEDIUM	793
V	SHADED GREEN	125
3	JADE – V. DARK	561
Y	JADE – MEDIUM	562
B'ST	ROYAL BLUE – DARK	796
=	JADE – LIGHT	563

BACKSTITCH ON PRAM — 725.

BACKSTITCH SPOKES ON PRAM, TRICYCLE. PEDALS ON TRICYCLE, BIKE & ALL FRENCH KNOTS — 310.

BACKSTITCH ON TRICYCLE HANDLES & SEAT — 792.

BACKSTITCH ON BICYCLE HANDLES & SEAT — 561.

BACKSTITCH FOR FEET INDICATIONS, NUMBERS & "Ft" — 796.

BACKSTITCH INDICATIONS FOR INCHES — 561.

PLEASE NOTE: IN ORDER FOR THIS PIECE TO MEASURE CORRECTLY IT MUST BE STITCHED ON 14 COUNT FABRIC.

OPTIONAL BACKSTITCHING:

BICYCLE FRAME #561
BICYCLE WHEELS #451
TRICYCLE FRAME #792
TRICYCLE WHEELS #451 & #310
WAGON HANDLE #451 & #310
WAGON #347
WAGON WHEELS #310, #451 & #347
ALPHABETS #562
ALL OF PRAM #451

To everything
–3 ft. there is a season
and a time
for every purpose
under heaven
Adam Gabriel
Mauro
October 1ˢᵗ 1988

4
A Child's Own Sampler

As you stitch a special project you may find a curious child is eager to help you. By setting up a project for a child to do, you can provide a unique learning and sharing experience. Children love to be involved, especially in grown-ups' activities, and a sampler of his or her own will include a child in your stitching without hampering your progress. Together you will produce two pieces with names and dates, sentiment and designs, that will be gratifying to stitch now and enjoy later.

When choosing a sampler for a child to stitch, be sure to involve the child in some elements of the choice, whether it be the design itself, the colors, the fabric, or the ultimate goal (a framed piece for Grandpa, a pillow for Mother, a box top for a favorite teacher, or perhaps a wall hanging for the child's own room). Try to accept most, if not all, the child's preferences, even if the color scheme, for example, seems wild or the destination grandiose. Some children will be much more motivated by a project that reflects their choices rather than yours. Also choose fabric in a large count (5, 7, or 11), use perle cotton, rather than floss, and a large needle with a very blunt tip. When choosing a design or creating one, stick to distinctly contrasting colors, and avoid half, quarter, or backstitches. Remember, too, that children's attention spans are limited, and their sense of inadequacy sometimes exaggerated. Remain patient, speak calmly, and do not pursue the activity for more than fifteen minutes or so (unless the child becomes absorbed and seems happy to continue). Have a threader handy, and watch for tangled thread or loops on the back of the work. A common frustration for children is the predilection for thread to tangle, and this in itself can deter enjoyment or a project's completion.

Finally, do not criticize mistakes but rather point them out and offer to help undo them if possible or necessary. The most charming of the antique samplers we see today are those rendered by children, and they usually contain mistakes, so emphasize that mistakes are nothing to be miserable about. On the other hand, taking out and correcting mistakes may be very rewarding to some children and may contribute to the shared experience. Try to rely on your sense of who the child is and what gratifies that child.

Stitched by Me

SYMBOL	COLOR	DMC PERLE #5
X	RED	666
O	ORANGE	947
I	YELLOW	973
\	BLUE	798
•	GREEN	702
+	VIOLET	552

5
Family Samplers

To stitch a family sampler is to join an international tradition as old as samplers themselves. Often depicted in a tree motif, the names of several generations in a family make an intriguing historical piece. Modern family samplers vary only in the style and shapes of the motifs (and in some cases the colors available) but are similar to antiques, as they depict marriages, deaths, and births and relate a unique story that may be enjoyed and studied for generations.

Some samplers have room for adding names as new family members arrive or are joined in; others document a specific period. In planning a family sampler, do all the required research well in advance of stitching so that major compositional changes need not be made in the midst of a project. This avoids the tedium and danger of excessive ripping. (We always expect to do a little "unstitching," but rearranging elements should be done on paper first.)

Be sure to sign (or initial) and date a family sampler, or include dates with the names of the family members so that future admirers will know what period of time the design refers to. The full names and dates of each person may not fit into designated spaces, but do try to include first initials and last names. Try to verify spelling before stitching—through the ages, unexpected name changes are more often attributed to spelling mistakes in family samplers (among other historical documents) than to intentional legal changes.

As with all finishing and framing, take care that the materials and techniques used in no way threaten the fibers of the worked piece. The method and materials used should always allow the piece to be completely undone and remounted without tearing, unraveling, or cutting. See Chapter 6 on framing and finishing to learn more about conservation mounting. This is important for all stitched work, but especially for family samplers.

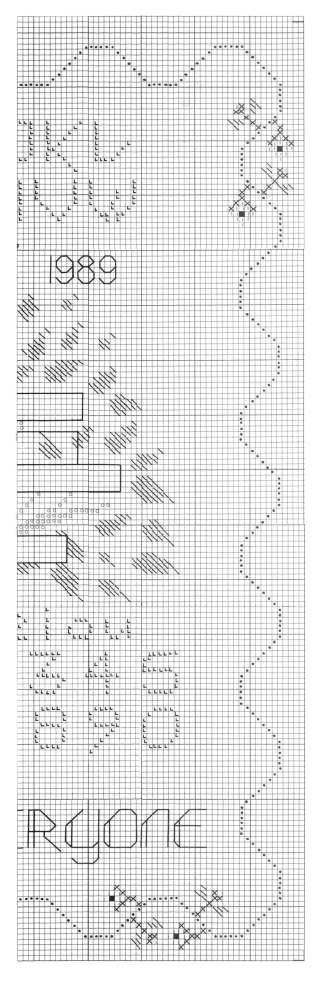

Family Tree

SYMBOL	COLOR	DMC#
\	GREEN GREY	3053
X	GREEN GREY—MED	3052
•	GREEN GREY—DARK	3051
▪	BLACK	310
I	SPORTSMAN FLESH—MED.	3064
L	GREY GREEN—MED.	927
O	DRAB BROWN—V. DARK	610
B'ST	BEAVER GREY	646

ALL BACKSTITCHING EXCEPT STITCHERS
INITIALS & YEAR IN BLACK #310.

STITCHERS INITIALS & YEAR—BEAVER GREY #646.

IN ORDER FOR THIS DESIGN TO BE WORKED
CORRECTLY, IT IS IMPORTANT THAT IT BE
STITCHED ON A LINEN OR LINEN-TYPE FABRIC
SO THAT STITCHES ARE WORKED OVER TWO
THREADS & THE LETTERING INSET IN THE
FAMILY MEMBERS' BOXES ARE HALF-SIZED,
WORKED OVER ONLY ONE THREAD.

81

6
Finishing Your Work

Great care should be taken in finishing and framing all stitched work. The material and techniques used should not in any way threaten the fibers used (both fabric and thread) or the piece's value. This means, in framing, that acid-free materials should be used; regular glass (not nonglare) should be used and should be removed from the work by "spacers"; air should be allowed to circulate freely within the piece (to prevent mildew); and the work should never be glued or fastened in any way that prevents the complete removal of all the framing materials. In other words, one should be able to take the framed or mounted piece apart and have an intact piece of needlework remain. Careful handling should allow a piece to be washed, remounted, or reframed without its raveling or falling apart because of cutting or gluing.

For pillows, bellpulls, wall hangings, and other forms of "soft" finishing, care should be taken to use cotton, silk, or wool fabrics and threads. Be sure to ask that colors be set before cleaning, and if you have any doubts, wash your piece yourself following the suggestions in Chapter 1.

Finally, make an effort to appreciate that the hours worked will be honored by quality finishing (professional or amateur) and that scrimping at the end will devalue your work.

7
Showing, Valuing, and Selling Your Work

Entering Fairs and Shows

Entering fairs and shows can be a very rewarding experience. Some are judged; others are not; a third group offers judging as an option. To enter work in any public forum, first get in touch with local recreation centers, churches, needlework guilds, county fairgrounds offices, and needlework stores and ask about shows and fairs. Entry blanks are usually available in advance and are required for entering work. Sometimes fees are charged either by piece or individual. Generally you should insure your own work, but often blanket insurance is provided (at a minimum value) by the exhibitor organization. The value of the piece should be estimated and noted when submitting a piece for exhibit, but be sure to check with your insurance agent to see if your work is covered outside your residence.

Before completing an entry blank, read it several times. Some questions may be ambiguous, and you should check them with the organization. Be as accurate as you can when describing your submissions and answer honestly when space is provided for description as original or not. Lack of originality is not penalized; it is usually entered in a separate category. Be sure to think about the "professional" category—it usually covers anyone who has been paid to stitch as well as those who have sold their work, who work in needlework stores, or who teach. If you do not know the design or origin of the piece, indicate so, do not make something up. Most organizations offer various categories into which they will place submitted work. In some cases you will determine the category (by filling out the form); otherwise your work will be designated as a certain kind and entered into a category.

Although judges are usually rigorously selected and meet high standards of professionalism and experience, when work is judged, many factors are weighed. Often, to the inexperienced eye, the judging may be difficult to understand. Usually knowing the category helps in understanding the judging, but judges' remarks are available and may be studied for more enlightenment. Do not feel reluctant or shy about querying the results. You will learn a great deal about technique and materials and presentation. Above all, do not feel slighted or wounded if all your pieces do not receive blue ribbons; the fun and reward of entering a show are in the education for everyone. Exposure to others' work, both for you and for those who see your work, enhances your appreciation and widens your horizons.

There is much to be learned at every level, and the more we see, the more eager we become to use different ideas, fibers, and techniques. Often shows and exhibits raise funds for worthwhile organizations—in addition they raise our awareness of the whole realm of stitching and inspire us to continue to explore.

Appraising, Insuring, and Selling Stitched Work

In order to insure a stitched sampler, one must know the value. This is difficult to determine in many cases, both for the amateur and even at times for the professional. For contemporary work, insurance usually covers the value of the materials used in stitching and in finishing or framing. Save your receipts from every step of your project, or if given a sampler, ask the material value, if you need to insure it. (If you feel reluctant to query the giver, ask a yarn store to estimate the value of the materials used.) The number of hours spent in work cannot be insured.

Antique samplers and some exceptional contemporary pieces need appraisal in order to be insured. Do not ask needlework-shop owners to appraise work. Instead use the services of professional appraisers acquainted with needlework. To find one, use the Yellow Pages or ask at a needlework shop. Be sure to ask the appraiser's fee before arranging an appointment. Quite often a fee will include the appraisal of several pieces, and you may economize by having several things appraised at one time. Submit a copy of the appraiser's paperwork to your insurance company, and be sure to photograph or videotape pieces of value.

Two factors are important when arriving at a price for work being sold; these are intrinsic worth and what the market will bear. Sometimes these two values conflict with each other, and a decision needs to be made about compromising one for the other. Appraised value is not necessarily an indication of price, and hours worked cannot be valued easily or accurately. The price you come up with should reflect the cost of the materials plus an amount for the complexity and the originality of the piece. However, selling work is difficult at best and very disappointing at worst. Make a decision before you price a piece about whether or not the price is negotiable, and if it is, acknowledge the lowest offer you can accept. Having made this decision, you need not apologize later.

To evaluate what the market will bear, visit galleries, fairs, or shops where comparable work is available for purchase. Above all, try to remove yourself from the piece, once you have priced it and made it available.

Appendix I
Alphabets and Border Designs

To complete your sampler with a child's name, the names of family members, dates or other figures, and your own initials or name, you need to have entire alphabets and figures at your fingertips. In the following pages, we have provided these for you, identifying them by the title of the pieces in which they appear.

Before you start, carefully count the stitches for this lettering. By considering the placement before you stitch, you will create a more effective piece and avoid having to rip out the personalized portions of your sampler. Perhaps you will want to chart the lettering before you pick up your needle.

The border that surrounds your work can strongly influence the entire piece. Where appropriate, our finished samplers show a border that complements the design. You may wish to interchange those already shown or use one of the nine additional borders in this section.

Early in your planning, make decisions about the border:

1. Do you want to use one?
2. Do you want to use the border shown in our finished piece?
3. Do you want to change the border? If so, which one will complement the style of your sampler? Will it successfully outline and define it? Will it fit the size of this piece? If you alter the borders, what color scheme will you work it in?

Make these decisions before you start to stitch, since they will influence the size of your design and the amount of thread you need to work it.

The borders provided here show you the corner of the piece, so you will know how they should meet. When you decide which to use, be sure you count carefully from the center of the larger design, so that the corners will meet properly. By working from the center, you can make certain the border edges will fall in the right place.

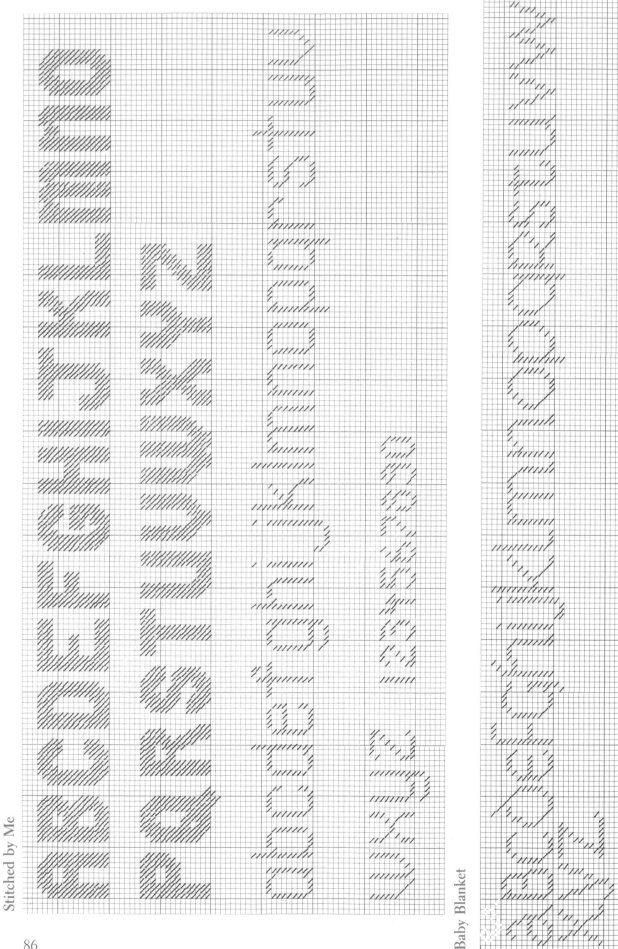

Baby Blanket

Family Tree and a Babe in the House

Little Lamb

Growth Chart

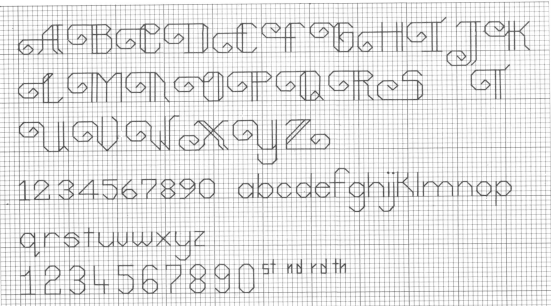

A House

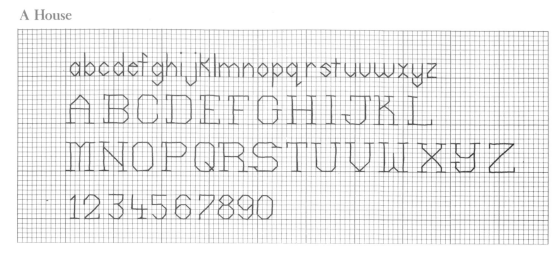

Family Tree

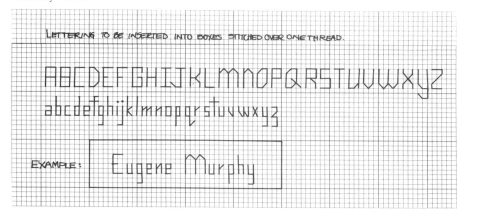

Baby's Awake, Baby's Asleep

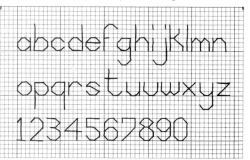

Pippa Passes

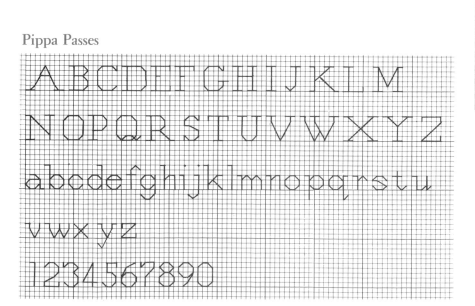

A Babe in a House

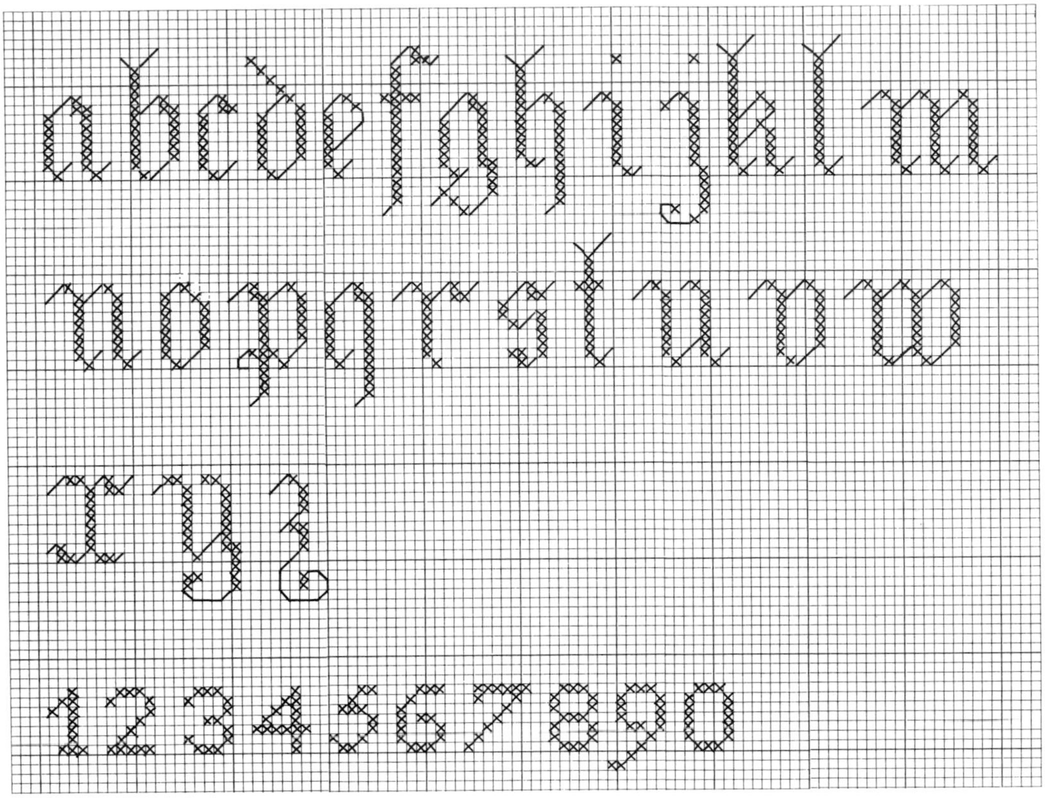

a b c d e f g h i j k l m
n o p q r s t u v w
x y z
1 2 3 4 5 6 7 8 9 0

All Things

A B C D E F G H I J K L M N O
P Q R S T U V W X Y Z
1 2 3 4 5 6 7 8 9 0

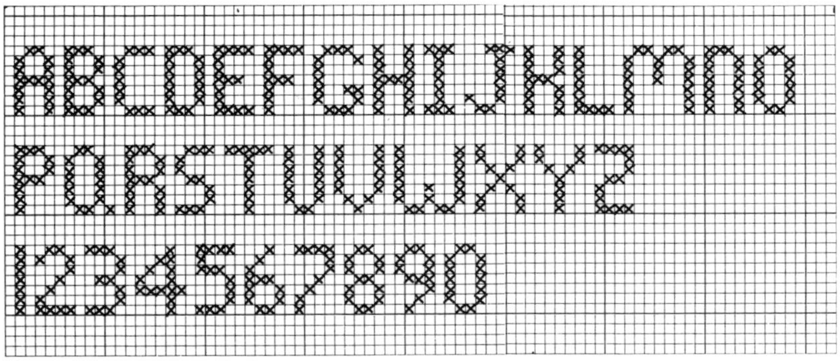

Train Up a Child

Aa Bb Cc Dd Ee Ff Gg Hh Ii Jj
Kk Ll Mm Nn Oo Pp Qq Rr
Ss Tt Uu Vv Ww Xx Yy Zz
1 2 3 4 5 6 7 8 9 0

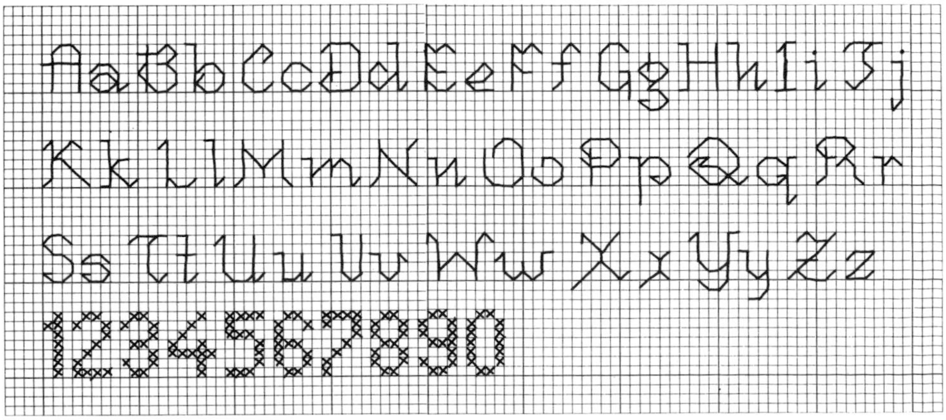

Appendix II
Learning More About
Needlework

As you become involved in needlework, you may wish to contact other people who are involved in it or discover new patterns and information. To help you, we have provided the following list of organizatins and publications.

Organizations

Many towns and cities have informal stitching groups, comprised of friends who regularly gather and stitch. Ask your needlework shops and friends about local groups. Nationally there are several groups well worth joining, whose local chapters usually offer day and evening meeting times and classes. Among them are:

American Needlepoint Guild (ANG)
P. O. Box 62101
Houston, TX 77205

Embroiderers' Guild of America, Inc. (EGA)
200 Fourth Avenue
Louisville, KY 40202

National Standards Council of American Embroiderers (NSCAE)
P. O. Box 8578
Northfield, IL 60093–8578

Publications

The Athelstane Stitcher's News
Start Rt. Box 228
Athelstane, WI 54104

Counted Thread
3305 S. Newport St.
Denver, CO 80224

Counted X-Stitch & Candlewick
P. O. Box 337
Seabrook, NH 03874

Country Handcrafts
5400 S. 60th St.
Greendale, WI 53129

Creative Needle
3421 Devonshire Dr.
Birmingham, AL 35209

Cross Stitch & Country Crafts
1716 Locust St.
Des Moines, IA 50336

The Cross Stitcher
P. O. Box 10779
Jackson, MS 39209

Embroidery
P. O. Box 42B
East Molesey, Surrey KT8 9BB England

The Flying Needle
562 Pine Valley Rd.
Marietta, GA 30328

Just Cross Stitch
400 Riverhills Bus. Pk.
Birmingham, AL 35242

McCall's Needlework & Crafts
825 7th Ave.
New York, NY 10019

Needle & Thread
4949 Byers
Fort Worth, TX 76107

Needle Arts
200 4th Ave.
Louisville, KY 40202

Needlecraft for Today
810 7th Ave.
New York, NY 10019

Needlepoint News
Box 5967
Concord, CA 94524

Needlepointers
2431 Poe Lane
Petersburg, CA 23803

Needlewords
P. O. Box 465
Pawleys Island, SC 29585

The Needlework Times
Suite 1405
6 N. Michigan
Chicago, IL 60602

Stitches Count
8991 Jane Road N.
Lake Elmo, MN 55042

Threads
63 S. Main St.
Newton, CT 06470

The Workbasket
4251 Pennsylvania
Kansas City, MO 64111

Appendix III
Suppliers and Supplies

Write to the following wholesale suppliers for information regarding where, in your area, to buy the supplies used in this book:

Wholesaler	Supplies Used
Wichelt R. R. 1 Stoddard, WI 54648	Cross-stitch fabric (Valentina)
Fleur de Paris 5835 Washington Boulevard Culver City, CA 90230	Floss, perle cotton, cross-stitch fabric
American Crewel & Canvas Studio 164 Canal Street P. O. Box 453 Canastota, NY 13032	Medici, cross-stitch fabric
Bernat Depot & Mendon Streets Uxbridge, MA 01569	Floss and perle cotton
Craft World 1301 Avondale Road New Windsor, MD 21776	Floss, perle cotton, cross-stitch fabric
Kreinik Mfg. Co. 1708 Gihon Road P. O. Box 1966 Parkersburg, WV 26101	Balger metallic thread

Eva Rosenstand Corp.
P. O. Box 185
Clovis, CA 93613-0185

Flower thread

List of Supplies Used, By Project

All Things
18-count ivory Aida
DMC floss

Baby Blanket
14-count Valentina fabric
DMC floss

Pippa Passes
14-count Rustico
DMC floss

Baby's Awake, Baby's Asleep
14-count navy Aida, powder-blue Aida
Balger metallic blending filament
DMC floss

A Babe in a House
30-count white linen
DMC floss

Family Tree
26-count sand linen
DMC floss

Block House
25-count "dirty" linen
DMC floss

Little Lamb
32-count Belfast linen
Eva Rosenstand flower thread

Stitched by Me
11-count white Aida
DMC perle #5

Growth Chart
14-count wheat Ragusa
DMC floss

Train Up a Child
Loomspun
DMC floss

Bibliography

Books

Bishop, Robert, and Secord, William. *Quilts, Coverlets, Rugs and Samplers.* The Knopf Collector's Guide to American Antiques. New York: Alfred A. Knopf, 1982.

Cavanaugh, J. Albert. *Lettering and Alphabets.* New York: Dover Publications, 1946.

Cirker, Blanche, ed. *Needlework Alphabets and Designs.* New York: Dover Publications, 1975.

Colby, Averil. *Samplers.* Newton, Mass.: Charles T. Branford Co., 1965.

DaBoll, Raymond. *Twentieth Edition Speedball Book.* Philadelphia: Hunt Manufacturing Co., 1972.

Don, Sarah. *Traditional Samplers.* New York: Viking/Penguin, Inc., 1986.

Dressman, Cecile. *Samplers for Today.* New York: Van Nostrand Reinhold Co., 1972.

Eaton, Jan, and Mundle, Liz. *Cross Stitch and Sampler Book.* New York: Sterling Publishing Co., 1985.

Fawday, Marguerite, and Brown, Deborah. *The Book of Samplers.* New York: St. Martin's Press, 1980.

Hurt, Zuelia Ann. *Country Samplers.* Birmingham, Ala.: Oxmoor House, Inc., 1984.

Kay, Dorothea. *Embroidered Samplers.* New York: Charles Scribner's Sons, 1975.

Lammer, Jutta. *Making Samplers—New and Traditional Designs.* New York: Sterling Publishing Co., 1984.

Sebba, Ann. *Samplers: Five Centuries of a Gentle Craft.* New York: Thames & Hudson, Inc., 1979.

Thompson, Ginnie. *Linen Stitches.* Sumter, S.C.: Designs by Gloria & Pat, Inc., 1987.

Wilson, Erica. *Erica Wilson's Children's World: Needlework Ideas From Children's Classics.* New York: Charles Scribner's Sons., 1983.

Wright, Harry B. *Lettering.* New York: Pitman Publishing Corp., 1967.

Leaflets and Magazines

The Alphabet Book. Leaflet 457. Little Rock, Ark.: Leisure Arts.

Barbara Cocherham, "Samplers: Threads of History." *Craft and Needlework Age* (January 1988).

Conley, Laura J. *Alphabets and Borders.*

A Cross Stitch Lesson for Beginners. Sumter, S.C.: Designs by Gloria & Pat, Inc.

"Fine and Rare Needleworks." *The Scarlet Letters Catalogue* 6.

George, Ross F. *Speedball Textbook for Pen and Brush Lettering.* Camden, N.J.: C. Howard Hunt Pen Co., 1960.

The Irving Munson Alphabet Book. Winston-Salem, N.C.: Jean Farish Needleworks.

Jean Farish Needleworks Abcedary. Winston-Salem, N.C.: Jean Farish Needleworks.

The Jean Farish Needleworks Alphabet Treasury. Winston-Salem, N.C.: Jean Farish Needleworks.

Just Cross Stitch (Jan.–Feb. 1988).

Popkin, Barbara. *Alphabetically Speaking.*

Tew, Harriet. *Script Alphabets.*

Thompson, Ginnie. *Teach Yourself Counted Cross Stitch.* Little Rock, Ark.: Leisure Arts.